THRIVE ONLINE

OTHER BOOKS IN THE THRIVE ONLINE SERIES

The Productive Online and Offline Professor: A Practical Guide

Bonni Stachowiak

Series Foreword by Kathryn E. Linder

Foreword by Robert Talbert

THRIVE ONLINE

A New Approach to Building Expertise and Confidence as an Online Educator

Shannon Riggs

Series Foreword by Kathryn E. Linder
Foreword by Penny Ralston-Berg

STERLING, VIRGINIA

COPYRIGHT © 2019 BY STYLUS PUBLISHING, LLC.

Published by Stylus Publishing, LLC.
22883 Quicksilver Drive
Sterling, Virginia 20166-2019

Names: Riggs, Shannon, 1970- author.
Title: Thrive online : a new approach to building expertise and confidence as an online educator / Shannon Riggs.
Description: First edition. | Sterling, Virginia : Stylus, 2019. | Includes bibliographical references and index.
Identifiers: LCCN 2017059441 (print) | LCCN 2018013528 (ebook) | ISBN 9781620367452 (Library networkable e-edition) | ISBN 9781620367469 (Consumer e-edition) | ISBN 9781620367445 (pbk. : alk. paper) | ISBN 9781620367438 (cloth : alk. paper)
Subjects: LCSH: Web-based instruction. | Internet in higher education. | Web-based instruction. | College teaching.
Classification: LCC LB2395.7 (ebook) | LCC LB2395.7 .R55 2019 (print) | DDC 378.1/7344678--dc23
LC record available at https://lccn.loc.gov/2017059441

13-digit ISBN: 978-1-62036-743-8 (cloth)
13-digit ISBN: 978-1-62036-744-5 (paperback)
13-digit ISBN: 978-1-62036-745-2 (library networkable e-edition)
13-digit ISBN: 978-1-62036-746-9 (consumer e-edition)

Printed in the United States of America

All first editions printed on acid-free paper that meets the American National Standards Institute Z39-48 Standard.

First Edition, 2019

This book is dedicated to the online educators with whom I have had the privilege to work, and to my family, who have supported me in the pursuit of my dreams, online and off.

TABLE OF CONTENTS

SERIES FOREWORD

The field of online teaching and learning has never been more exciting than it is right now. Technology and tools are catching up to our vision for access and improving student learning. Online learning innovations are happening daily, bringing new opportunities for engaging our students and meeting the needs of today's learners.

It is because of the constantly evolving landscape of online higher education that online instructors and stakeholders need a book series that is just for them, one that provides a positive view of online teaching and is full of practical tips and suggestions to make their professional lives easier, more rewarding, and more respected. Thrive Online is that series.

The Thrive Online series was designed to focus on the needs, interests, and best practices of instructors teaching online with the ultimate goal of helping to better serve online students.

In this title book of the Thrive Online series, Shannon Riggs demonstrates the skills and tools needed to create engaging learning experiences for online students, while also articulating methods online instructors can use to embrace and thrive in their careers.

Riggs's history as an online instructor and an instructional designer, as well as her current experience as one of the leaders of Oregon State University's top-ranked and award-winning Ecampus online programs, have contributed to her vast knowledge of the culture and best practices of online education.

I asked Riggs to contribute to this series because she knows what it takes to create online learning experiences that will transform learners. She also sees the dedicated faculty and staff working behind the scenes to create these transformative online experiences. From the instructors, to the instructional designers, to the multimedia developers, to the student support personnel, to the advisers, and all the other amazing online administration professionals in between, Riggs illustrates how it really does take a village to ensure that students will have an optimal learning experience online.

Through this first book launching the Thrive Online series, I am excited to continue the conversation about what makes online learning such a rich experience. Future books in the series will also contribute important elements to this conversation. Each of the contributors to the Thrive Online series are fearless, committed thought leaders who have embraced distance education and believe it is not only the *future* of higher education but also the *now* of the teaching and learning landscape.

I hope you will join the conversation using #ThriveOnline to share your own experiences in the online teaching and learning landscape as we continue to grow the community of committed and passionate online learning advocates in higher education. Come thrive with us!

Kathryn E. Linder
Series Editor
February 2019

FOREWORD

Since its inception, we've seen many different iterations of online learning. New online course designers and creators often attempted to replicate what happens in the classroom. When faced with a new challenge, it's a natural reaction to go with what you know. Lectures were recorded and streamed to online students or transcribed into text for students to read online. This met the immediate need for access—online students received equivalent content and materials as their face-to-face counterparts—but did it truly address learning?

As time passed, Internet bandwidth grew. Then came a trend toward raising "engagement," with an emphasis on media and technology. Many course designers and creators incorporated more graphics, media, and interactive pieces to make courses less text based and more engaging—often mistaking excitement and higher production value for genuine learner engagement. High production value content, when only watched, is still passive learning.

This brings us to the present day. The variety of tools available to create, enhance, and deliver online learning have grown dramatically. Course designers and creators can be overwhelmed with options and find it difficult to sort through the possibilities to find the most effective solutions.

Student demographics in higher education have also changed. Higher Learning Advocates (2017) reports the average age of students is increasing, more students work while going to school, and many are financially independent—meaning they are responsible for paying for their own education. More students than ever before are taking online courses. More universities are offering online courses. At the same time, students are expecting more from their online courses.

The convergence of increased student need for courses, increased student expectations of courses, increased competition among course providers, and increased possibilities for what courses can be means quality teaching and learning is more important than ever before. In a world of possibilities, outcomes are key. Do students learn by doing? Does the coursework produce tangible artifacts to prove competency to potential employers? Are students actively engaged with their course instructor, content, and classmates? Are they actively reflecting and thinking? Or are they passively trudging through busy work?

Enter Shannon Riggs. I have witnessed firsthand Shannon's commitment to quality teaching and learning for the benefit of all students, and this text is an extension of those values and beliefs. With her vast experience and deep expertise in different aspects of teaching, learning, instructional design, and leadership in higher education, she is uniquely poised to help all of us thrive in this world of online teaching and learning possibilities.

The timeliness of this text is uncanny. Riggs has brought the most important aspects of online learning—and all teaching and learning for that matter—to light. The text represents a thorough understanding of common misconceptions and pitfalls as well as the effective strategies needed to create a meaningful and valued learning experience. In one concise volume, she provides the necessary tools for course designers and creators to become fully fluent in active learning strategies.

This book is no passive read. Riggs encourages readers to reflect on and refine their teaching practices all along the way. It is a journey—an active learning experience for the reader. The ideas sparked by this text through the use of the #ThriveOnline hashtag in social media will provide benefits beyond these pages by creating an active professional learning community.

Whether you find yourself critical, curious, or already committed to online learning, you will find benefit in this text and the #ThriveOnline experience.

Penny Ralston-Berg
Chair, Quality Matters Instructional Designers Association
Senior Instructional Designer,
Pennsylvania State University World Campus

PREFACE

I began my career teaching college writing in traditional face-to-face classrooms. Even then, when people were still using dial-up modems to access the Internet, I used online components in my course designs. In my very first class at Thomas Nelson Community College in Hampton, Virginia, my students used electronic mailing lists to share reflections on assigned readings and to exchange feedback on essay drafts. At the time, my husband was pursuing a career in the U.S. Navy and our children were in preschool and elementary school. The Navy carried our family through 15 relocations in the last 17 years of my husband's 20-year career. This meant a lot of job searching for me, which ultimately led to teaching opportunities in community colleges and in private and public colleges and universities all over the United States and in Canada, both online and off.

Early in my career, after one poorly timed move left me without teaching work for a semester, I tapped into my stores of Navy-spouse practicality and said to myself, "I am good with technology. I think I will try this online teaching thing." To be honest, I did not expect to enjoy it, because I loved being in the classroom. And, I am not ashamed to admit that I had my doubts about whether I could teach online as well as I could in the classroom. Because of the job portability online teaching afforded, and because we had quite a few more Navy-related moves ahead of our family, I was motivated to try it.

Over the years, I discovered that I actually enjoyed more one-on-one interactions with more individual students online than I was ever able to manage in the classroom. Furthermore, the interactions I had with my students online tended to be more substantive, regular, and transformative for students in comparison with my face-to-face attempts at teaching. In the classroom, I had success engaging confident, extroverted students—those who sit in the front and center of the classroom. The quieter, seemingly less confident students who actually comprised the majority were much more difficult to engage, though I tried hard. Online, though, because I designed my courses to require participation and interaction, I found that I heard from the quiet majority far more often than I was able to on campus. And, because I could engage with them more, I had more of an impact on their developing skills as writers. I became a believer in online education.

Success in online teaching led to opportunities in course design and development; faculty development; instructional design; and, ultimately, leadership roles. Regardless of my role, in working shoulder to shoulder and screen to screen with other online educators, I have too often heard colleagues express feelings of being unseen, unrecognized, and undervalued for their work in online education. Though I have had the pleasure of working at several institutions that value and support online education and educators, I have been no stranger to suggestions from colleagues less experienced with online education that online courses are easier, less rigorous, or otherwise not as good as traditional face-to-face courses. In my own online teaching and in helping others with their online teaching work, however, I have witnessed countless creative, challenging course designs and the work of hundreds of devoted, engaged educators.

Recognizing, replicating, inspiring, and supporting the good work of online educators, for me, has been a source of great joy in my instructional design, faculty development, and leadership work. This book is a natural extension of that work and is an attempt to help others experience the joy of a thriving career in online education.

A FEW WORDS ABOUT ONLINE EDUCATION

In the long history of higher education, online education is still quite new, and, as such, the vocabulary used to discuss it is not always consistent. When professionals in higher education use the term *online education* they may be referring to a wide variety of teaching environments and methods—for example, synchronous teaching conducted via Web-conference; self-paced, nonfacilitated computerized learning; or on-demand educational resources that happen to be available on the Internet.

This book, however, is about a specific kind of online teaching and learning: facilitated, asynchronous online education in which an educator guides students to progress through a course of study in asynchronous but regular communication with each other. This book will also be helpful for those teaching hybrid or blended courses, in which courses are delivered using a combination of online and in-class activities, especially where the online activities are asynchronous and facilitated. This book will not directly address other forms of education conducted online, though readers engaged in those kinds of enterprises will likely find useful takeaways.

MY HOPE FOR THIS BOOK

My hope for this book is that you will not only read it but also engage with it and join the community of online educators eager to change the conversation about online education. The work you are doing matters, and your voice and perspective need to be heard. By designing and teaching online courses, you are educating students who might otherwise go unserved, enabling them to improve their economic opportunities, their minds, their lives, and the lives of the generations who will follow. Furthermore, the work you are doing is slowly but surely changing not just *online* teaching and learning, but *all* teaching and learning. As students and faculty move between online and traditional learning environments, evolutionary steps forward in one learning modality traverse into others.

By reflecting on your own work as an online educator, I hope you will discover strategies to improve your professional well-being and hope that you will thrive in your career. Throughout the book, you will find questions for reflection to help you apply the concepts discussed to your own professional context and situation. Every institution is different, and online educators, as a community of practice, have many different career paths and goals. Carefully working through these questions will help you bring ideas from this book to fruition in your institutional context and professional life.

As you read this book, you will likely find it helpful to keep a paper or an electronic journal or to create a blog where you can share your reflections more publicly and invite others in your network to participate in the changing conversation. You may also want to share brief reflections and epiphanies with tweets, Facebook posts, or captioned images on Instagram. Therefore, throughout this book, in addition to Invitations to Connect, you will also find Invitations to Reflect with the community of other online educators sharing this journey with you via social media using the hashtag #ThriveOnline.

Furthermore, I hope this book will be read and discussed by groups of faculty, staff, faculty development professionals, administrators, community and corporate partners, students, and all who work to improve access to educational opportunities through online education. The heart of this book is about the real human connections being made in fully online, asynchronous courses; about shifting higher education to be more inclusive of the faculty members who are engaged in this important work; and about helping online educators find ways to thrive in their careers.

ACKNOWLEDGMENTS

Despite long hours alone in the study, no book is written in isolation. This one is no different. I am grateful to Ariel Anbar of Arizona State University, Thomas Cavanagh of the University of Central Florida, and Laura Pasquini of the University of North Texas for agreeing to be interviewed for this book. Their perspectives and insights have enriched my understanding. GwenEllyn Anderson of Chemeketa Community College and Mary Bucy of Western Oregon University were also extraordinarily helpful in the planning stages for this book.

I am also grateful to have worked for two truly inspiring and innovative leaders in online education, Loraine Schmitt, dean of distance education for Portland Community College in Portland, Oregon, and Lisa Templeton, associate provost for the Division of Extended Campus at Oregon State University. Lessons I have learned from them appear throughout. Sarah Burrows has also influenced the writing of this book with her thoughtful feedback, probing questions, and genuine excitement about the future of online education and educators.

I once received a comment on a teaching evaluation from a student in an online technical writing course. The student wrote, "I have never felt so good about working so hard." It was the best professional compliment of my teaching career, and it expresses exactly how I feel about my colleague and editor, Katie Linder, who models what it means to thrive. Every writer should be so fortunate as to have such a fiercely intelligent, driven, and discerning editor, colleague, and friend.

PART ONE

CHANGING THE CONVERSATION

CHANGING THE CONVERSATION

The work of online educators is often engaging, creative, and deeply rewarding. Online educators are bringing education to students who would not otherwise have access, and student demand for online education is clearly on the rise. In a recent study, 28% of students reported taking at least 1 online course, with about half of those students seeking their degrees fully online (Allen, Seaman, Poulin, & Straut, 2016). Beyond the satisfaction of reaching greater numbers of students, connecting personally with individual students, cultivating and observing students' growth, and bearing witness to students' "aha!" moments are some of the greatest joys of the teaching life. Many dedicated online educators know the experience of basking in the glow of a laptop screen, filled with the satisfaction of knowing they have made a difference.

In these intimate teaching moments, it is easy for online educators to understand why the research shows that online courses demonstrate no significant difference in student attainment of learning outcomes in comparison with traditional face-to-face courses; in fact, online students have performed modestly better than their counterparts in traditional face-to-face classes, likely because they spend more time on task (U.S. Department of Education, 2010). A recent survey found that more than 70% of academic leaders recognized that learning outcomes in online courses were the same or superior to those in face-to-face courses; however, only 29.1% of chief academic officers in the same survey reported that their faculty perceive online education as valuable and legitimate (Allen et al., 2016). Though student demand for online education is strong, many educators appear to be conflicted, some still questioning the value and legitimacy of online education and others embracing the opportunity to reach more students and master new ways of teaching.

In almost two decades of experience working in higher education, I have encountered both these points of view and have helped faculty navigate the spaces in between. Some faculty come to online teaching from a place of curiosity. They want to experiment with teaching in a new environment and with new technologies. Interestingly, in the last couple of years, I have worked with a few faculty members who have come to online teaching because of their own experiences as online students. They have shared that online education made attaining their degrees possible, and that they have come to online teaching motivated to reach students who need the accessibility to education that online courses provide. Faculty with experience as online students have certainly not comprised the majority of my experience, but as more and more students seek online education opportunities at the undergraduate and graduate levels, I look forward to this trend growing over time and to exploring how this student perspective will affect teaching practices.

Far more often, I have worked with faculty new to online education, and while some arrive eager to expand their teaching repertoires and curious about new methods of teaching, more arrive with uncertainty, doubt, and reservations. Over the years, I have observed these reservations expressed in several guises: misconceiving online education as a form of correspondence or computer-based learning courses that lack interaction and meaningful engagement; believing that online education is only suitable in certain disciplines; categorizing online education as a second-best alternative for students unable to attend face-to-face classes on campus; believing that online courses are less rigorous academically; and feeling a lack of confidence in the ability to connect with students online in the ways necessary for good teaching. Table 1.1 outlines some common misconceptions about online education, where those misconceptions may have originated, and some perspectives about the reality of online education today.

Some online faculty developers and instructional designers find misconceptions, doubts, and reservations frustrating. With experience, I have come to see these as useful places to begin because they are rooted in the practices and values of good teaching:

TABLE 1.1

Common Misconceptions About Online Education

Common misconceptions about online education	Possible origins of the misconceptions	Realities of online education today
"Online courses are easier and less rigorous than face-to-face courses."	• Some educators may have seen early or poorly designed and facilitated online courses in the past. • Others have difficulty understanding how student-content, student-student, and student-instructor interaction works in online courses due to lack of training and experience.	Poorly designed and facilitated courses exist online and on campus. If an educator is committed to providing a high-quality, rigorous learning experience for students, the educator can do so online just as well as can be done on campus, though it may take some additional professional development for the educator to learn how to design and facilitate online courses well.

| "More students cheat or plagiarize in online courses than in traditional settings." | • Based on their experiences using educational technology for on-campus courses, some may think of the learning management system as a document repository rather than as a flexible learning environment with many instructional capabilities.
• Some educators believe that the online environment creates a false sense of anonymity that can tempt students to cheat because they think they have less chance of being caught.
• Others think that the copy-and-paste functions available on computers and other devices invite sloppy habits that lead to academic integrity violations. | Study results are mixed. Some say more cheating happens online, others say more cheating happens on campus, and others find no significant difference. Regardless of the modality of instruction, educators should recognize the following:
• Virtually all students have easy access to information on the Internet, so meeting face-to-face alone does not protect against integrity violations.
• Teaching students to behave ethically in general academic and discipline-specific contexts requires effort and is part of our responsibility as educators. |

(Continues)

Table 1.1 (*Continued*)

Common misconceptions about online education	Possible origins of the misconceptions	Realities of online education today
		• The most effective protections against academic integrity violations are well-designed assignments and assessments.
"I will not be able to connect meaningfully with my students."	• Recalling correspondence courses or confusing facilitated, computer-based online education with self-paced nonfacilitated learning may lead some not to realize the fullness and complexity of online teaching and learning.	• To qualify for federal financial aid, institutions must offer online courses that meet rigorous standards for facilitation and interaction. Meaningful teaching and learning happen in online courses every day but do not happen automatically. Educators need to design and facilitate courses well to create and encourage meaningful learning experiences.

recognition of the importance of learning communities; a desire to help students master the specific knowledge, skills, and habits of mind of a given discipline; a desire for students to have the best possible educational experience and not settle for second best; a commitment to preserving academic rigor and integrity; and a desire to preserve the tradition of human connection central to the teaching and learning experience. When I encounter these doubts and misconceptions in the faculty I work with, I have learned to recognize them as foundations because I know that together we can build on them with effective course designs, pedagogical approaches, and teaching practices that make for well-designed and facilitated online courses.

INVITATION TO REFLECT: IMPLEMENTING ACTIVE LEARNING ONLINE

1. For those who are fairly new to online education, do you share some of the doubts, misconceptions, or reservations discussed here?
2. For those who are more experienced in online education, do you recall feeling reservations or believing misconceptions such as these? How did those feelings and beliefs change over time?

Invitation to Connect

Join the Thrive Online community. Share your thoughts using #ThriveOnline.

Over the years, in helping faculty members overcome reservations about online education, I have found myself returning to the useful phrase, "when designed well." When designed well, online courses foster robust learning communities where students interact with the content, with other students, and with the faculty member on a regular basis throughout the course. When designed well, any discipline can be taught online with academic rigor and integrity. When designed well, instructional faculty can connect meaningfully with students in all the ways necessary for good teaching. This phrase has been useful because it acknowledges that faculty may have witnessed poorly designed online education in the past, perhaps in online education's early days, in a workplace training module, or from an institution where online course development and teaching are not well supported. This phrase also signals that I am committed to providing high-quality educational experiences, that I am someone who shares the value of good teaching, and that I am not daunted by the hard work delivering high-quality online education requires. Perhaps most importantly, the phrase "when designed well" changes the conversation. We set aside the discussion of *whether* online education can be done well, and we begin a new dialogue about *how to do it well*.

As we change the conversation, it can be helpful to acknowledge that good teaching does not spring naturally from a particular modality. A good course on campus is not good because of the location or traditional brick-and-mortar ambiance. Likewise, a weak online course is not weak because it is delivered via the Internet.

Good teaching does not spring naturally from a particular modality.

#ThriveOnline

Good teaching in any learning environment requires careful attention to course design and facilitation.

As you gain experience with online teaching, you will find what generations of traditional classroom teachers have found. That is, investing time and effort in building quality course designs and improving teaching practices will lead to effective, satisfying educational experiences for you and your students. This book seeks to help online educators build confidence in their teaching through the following: exploring practices that lead to well-designed and facilitated online courses, encouraging self-assessment and reflection about online teaching knowledge and skills, highlighting the unique advantages afforded by the online medium, and exploring the changing role of educators and how to find professional satisfaction in such a time of change. Finally, this book seeks to help online educators and higher education professionals at all levels move beyond the question of *whether* college teaching can be conducted online at all and beyond the misconceptions that overlook the incredible work, accomplishments, and success stories that are taking place every day in the field of online learning. Today's practitioners can be confident that online courses, when designed and facilitated well, do lead to successful outcomes. What we are more interested in now is a new approach to the conversation, one that moves beyond misconceptions and beyond attempts to demonstrate equivalency to traditional on-campus education—a new approach that helps us discover the many ways we can *thrive online.*

COMPARING LEARNING ENVIRONMENTS

When starting out in online education, as with any new adventure, before we can excel and thrive, first we need to get the lay of the land. In the world of online education, this means understanding the ways the online environment is similar to the face-to-face environment and the ways it is different. For those curious about online education, this process of discovery can be intriguing and exciting. For those who may have reservations or doubts about the quality of online educational experiences, considering the significant similarities between good face-to-face teaching and good online teaching can inspire confidence.

Course learning outcomes are one thing classes in both modalities should have in common. If an institution offers the same course on campus and online, students in both versions should be expected to meet the same learning outcomes, as would students who have enrolled in different sections of the same on-campus course taught by different instructors. When well designed and facilitated, online courses are not diluted or altogether different versions of their well-designed and facilitated campus-based counterparts.

The academic rigor of a well-designed online course should also be similar to the rigor required for the well-designed on-campus version of the same course. Online courses should not be easier. In fact, some students find online courses more challenging because they must be more disciplined about managing their time and limiting distractions. Many institutions use online learning readiness assessments to help students identify if they are up to the challenge of studying online. For example, the University of North Carolina at Chapel Hill's Online Learning Readiness Questionnaire (2010) helps students assess readiness in several categories including self-discipline, learning preferences, learning environment, computer literacy, and equipment.

Another way to measure rigor is by the number of credit hours for a course, as credit hours determine the approximate number of hours required for students to meet that course's learning outcomes. A common guideline for students is that each credit requires 1 hour of seat time and 2 to 3 hours of study time for an on-campus course. So, for a 3-credit course, students would attend class for 3 hours per week and study for 6 to 9 hours, for a total of 9 to 12 hours. Online, the seat time and study time are not distinct, but students should be spending the same total amount of time each week. In the example of the 3-credit online course, students should expect to spend 9 to 12 hours each week working on that course. Furthermore, as outlined by the course learning outcomes, the work itself should be similarly challenging, regardless of the modality. Additional factors that contribute to rigor in online courses are assessments, aligned in terms of content and cognitive level with learning outcomes; meaningful participation in a learning community; constructive feedback from the instructor on student work; and overall learner engagement. These factors will be discussed in greater detail later in this book.

Perhaps the most important similarity between the learning environments, though, is that good teaching online requires many of the same aptitudes and behaviors as good teaching on campus. Some faculty new to online education mistake online courses for computer-based learning, where students log into a system and interact only with content and assessments. Asynchronous online education is quite different from the computer-based learning one might find in workplace trainings, however, and from correspondence courses delivered in decades past. Well-designed and facilitated online courses involve interaction between not only students and the content but also students and other students as well as students and faculty members. In fact, distance education compliance requirements issued by the federal government (U.S. Department of Education, 2012) *require* that institutions offering online courses "support regular and substantive interaction between these students and the instructor" (p. 6). Failure to meet those compliance requirements make an institution ineligible for Title IV federal financial aid programs. Well-designed online courses that meet federally mandated definitions of *distance education* are highly interactive, with significant levels of communication required between faculty and students. Faculty beginning to teach online should expect a high degree of interaction with their students, perhaps even higher than they have experienced when teaching face-to-face courses.

DIFFERENCES BETWEEN THE LEARNING ENVIRONMENTS

While learning outcomes, academic rigor, and good teaching practices may be the same for online and on-campus courses, there are also some important differences to be aware of when transitioning from teaching on campus to online. For some faculty new to online education, the most surprising difference is in the workflow. Good online teaching requires two distinct bodies of work conducted in two discrete phases: developing the course materials, followed by conducting the course itself. Sometimes faculty new to online teaching resist the recommendation to separate these two bodies of work because they are typically conflated in on-campus teaching; therefore, approaching them separately may seem unnecessarily complicated and time consuming. However, because online course development requires significant amounts of writing course material, developing media, and building content and activities in a learning management system, attempting to develop and teach an online course simultaneously can quickly become overwhelming and can lead to poor quality design and teaching. See Box 1.1 for more on resources required to develop online courses.

Another difference between on-campus and online teaching is that training is often *required* for online teaching and course development. At many institutions offering online courses and programs, training in course design, educational technology, and pedagogy and best practices for online teaching is viewed not merely as helpful and nice to have, but mandatory. In fact, in addition

Box 1.1 Developing a New Online Course

How much time does online course development require?

Time commitments for developing a new online course vary based on a number of factors, including the faculty member's level of experience, whether the course has previously been taught in other formats, the degree of support available from the home institution, and the level of complexity of new multimedia components needed for the class. A useful guideline, however, is that the development of an online course is roughly equivalent to that of teaching one course.

How do institutions support faculty in online course development?

Support for online course development varies widely by institution. Some provide course development funding for overload pay or release time from teaching. Some provide compensation over the summer months for online course development. Some provide instructional design and multimedia development services, as well as training. Others sponsor or encourage mentoring programs. Support varies due to budget constraints and institutional priorities. Faculty new to online education would be wise to fully investigate available supports prior to embarking on the online course development journey.

to faculty academic credentials, training requirements for instructors to teach distance learners account for 20% of the U.S. News and World Report's ranking of online bachelor's degree programs (U.S. News and World Report, 2018). Though training does require additional time and effort, if designed well, it should help faculty be more prepared for online teaching and improve the quality of the educational experience for students and faculty alike.

Perhaps the most obvious difference as faculty transition from teaching on campus to online is that students will not be gathered together in one place and time to attend class with the instructor. In online classes, students will come and go throughout the week at all times of the day and night, participating in the course according to their own individual schedules. The flexibility afforded by online, asynchronous courses is what draws many students to online education to begin with, as it allows them to balance school with work, family, and other priorities. This flexibility can also be advantageous for busy faculty members who need to balance teaching with research, writing, field work, travel, and family commitments of their own.

Why is it important to understand that there are core similarities but critical differences between teaching on campus and online? In short, this helps us know that teaching well on campus does not mean that one will automatically be prepared to teach well online. Good online teaching requires some of the same core competencies as traditional campus-based teaching but calls for additional proficiencies as well.

In addition to appreciating the lay of the land externally in comparing learning environments, it is also important

Good online teaching requires some of the same core competencies as traditional campus-based teaching, but calls for additional proficiencies as well.

#ThriveOnline

to look inward. A self-study of your online course development and teaching practices will help you know your professional self more deeply and will help to illuminate the ways your online teaching practices can align with your values as an educator. Identifying your strengths and the competencies you have mastered can inspire confidence. Becoming aware of any weaknesses or potential areas for growth will help you know where to focus efforts to learn and improve. In many areas of our professional lives, clarifying our values and identifying how they align with our work provides direction and builds deep wells of confidence we can draw from in the virtual classroom and throughout our careers.

The remainder of Part One is intended to guide you through a reflective self-assessment of core abilities, skills, and competencies needed in online education. If you are new to online education, you should discover some useful fundamentals. If you have some experience with online education, as you read through each section, consider how your course development and teaching practices compare. You may find some ideas to sharpen your teaching skills. You may find descriptions of teaching practices you are currently using but perhaps were not fully conscious of. You may also become more aware of the values that drive your teaching.

TRAINING FOR ONLINE EDUCATORS

When assessing your knowledge and skill levels related to online teaching, it is helpful to begin by considering

---

Invitation to Connect
As you work through the remainder of Part One, share your reflections and epiphanies on social media and remember to use #ThriveOnline to join the community of other educators sharing this journey with you.

---

the topics on which you have already received training. At institutions where online education is well supported, the curriculum for new online educators can be quite robust and often includes course design and development outcomes. These outcomes often cover topics such as student-centered course organization and navigation; usability and understanding how people interact and operate in an online environment; alignment of learning outcomes, assessments, learning activities, and course materials; and outcomes-based development as opposed to textbook-driven development (see Table 1.2). The curriculum may also cover the presentation of content, such as when and how to use multimedia, how to organize and sequence lecture content for online asynchronous classes, how to find quality content online, how to create custom multimedia content, and how to write for the screen instead of the page. Design and development outcomes in educator training might also include discussion of the sequencing and pacing of content and assignments.

Online course design and development training may focus on considerations for creating course orientation documents, for example, establishing a course communication plan, including participation expectations for

TABLE 1.2
Training Needed for Online Course Design and Teaching

Training needed	Range of topics covered
Course design	Online course organization, alignment, content presentation, sequencing and pacing, course orientation, policies and support services, and legal considerations such as accessibility regulations and requirements of the Federal Educational Right to Privacy Act (FERPA)
Best practices in online teaching and pedagogy	Understanding online students; communication strategies for asynchronous courses; active learning; group work; project-based learning; pedagogical approaches such as cognitive behavioral, social constructionist, connectivist, or open; providing feedback; and differentiating instruction
Educational technology	Learning management system, plagiarism-prevention software, media systems, specialized software, social media and other Web-based technologies

students and preferred contact methods for the instructor; estimated response times for responding to questions and providing feedback on assignments; guidelines for online etiquette and policies; and information about how online students access student services such as the disability services office, advising, and tutoring. There are also the legalities of teaching online, such as how to use social media and remain compliant with the Federal Educational

Rights and Privacy Act (FERPA), copyright law as it pertains to online education, creative commons licensing, and accessibility requirements. Finally, course design and development training may offer tips for easing the maintenance workload when a developed course is taught repeatedly, such as using Week 1 or Week 2 in the course shell instead of specific dates.

Training for online educators can also include coverage of online pedagogical approaches and best practices for teaching online, such as understanding online students, who they are, and why they are taking online asynchronous courses; communicating effectively in an online asynchronous environment; doing active learning in an online environment; designing effective online group work; using project-based learning and staging projects for online learners; and implementing cognitive behavioral, social constructivist, connectivist, and open pedagogies. Additionally, training may include a discussion of how to provide meaningful feedback on student work in an online environment and how to differentiate instruction for specific student groups who may be behind or advanced.

Finally, training for online educators can include coverage of educational technologies, for example, how to upload files to the learning management system; how to build assignments and assessments; how to adjust settings for item availability and due dates; how to assign points to gradable items; how to organize and use the online grade book; how to format course pages so they are accessible and readable and meet usability standards; how students will interact with your particular learning management system; which paths are available to them; how and where to provide feedback on student work; and how to use other enterprise-wide technologies available on your campus. Those technologies may include plagiarism prevention software, media systems your institution has licensed that may be embedded in your learning management system, and specialized software systems in virtual labs, such as statistics or engineering programs.

Training programs and support for faculty teaching online vary widely by institution. Indeed, some institutions provide only limited training or no training at all. In those contexts, online educators often learn from written resources such as articles, books, or blogs; from more experienced colleagues or mentors; from formal or informal peer learning communities; or, simply from trial-and-error experience.

Invitation to Connect

Share your reflections with a community of online educators using #ThriveOnline.

ALIGNMENT

Perhaps the most critical competency for designing an online course prior to teaching is aligning the various components of the course. Educators use the term *alignment* to describe the degree to which course learning outcomes, assessments, learning activities, and course materials work together in terms of the topic's breadth and depth and

INVITATION TO REFLECT:
YOUR TRAINING FOR ONLINE COURSE DEVELOPMENT AND TEACHING

1. Does your institution offer training for online educators? If so, which topics are addressed?
2. Consider the following list of topics that are often included in training for new online educators. How would you rate your level of competency for each? In which areas might you want to learn more?

   a. Organization, navigation, and usability
   b. Developing policies for online classes
   c. Designing assessments for the online environment
   d. Alignment
   e. Multimedia use and development
   f. Sequencing and pacing content and assignments
   g. Online course facilitation
   h. Technical writing
   i. Legal considerations
   j. Pedagogical approaches
   k. Active learning
   l. Educational technology

3. Are there other competencies related to online teaching you have mastered? Are there other areas you are curious about or that you need more development in?

the cognitive level for the desired student mastery. In perhaps the most common approach to planning or assessing the alignment of a course, the learning outcomes are examined for the topics they represent, and they are classified according to Bloom's (1956) taxonomy of learning domains. Cognitive domains include lower level knowledge, comprehension, and application and higher levels of analysis, synthesis, and evaluation. When course components are aligned, the course is improved much the same way an essay is improved when the thesis is clear and the remainder of the essay supports it. The audience finds the message—in this case, the course as a whole—understandable, purposeful, and more impactful when alignment is in place. When alignment is lacking, the message becomes muddled, confusing, and unpersuasive.

Online educators must pay close attention to alignment and for very practical reasons. Without alignment, online courses can get bloated with extraneous content, bogging students down, or they can feel sparse, leaving students feeling lost or cheated out of a robust learning experience. Assessments can seem unfairly difficult or overly simple and pointless. Learning activities can feel like busy work because how they support learning outcomes is unclear. And students can leave a class with a successful grade yet be unable to articulate what they have actually learned. (These concerns certainly exist for traditional courses as well and represent one of the similarities between online and traditional learning environments.) The most well-respected and commonly used rubrics for evaluating online courses, including the Quality Matters (2018) rubric, the Online Learning Consortium's (2014) scorecard, and the Rubric for Online Instruction (California State University, Chico, 2016), all include alignment-related criteria.

Because online courses require so much writing and because they often require some professional development or the assistance of an instructional designer, online educators conduct extensive planning in a process commonly referred to as *backward design* to help achieve alignment in the design of a course (see Table 1.3.) The idea is to begin with the end in mind, to consider what the student learning outcomes need to be. From there, instructors determine what the appropriate summative assessments should be. If the learning outcomes correspond to the lower levels of Bloom's (1956) taxonomy, this might be a standard multiple-choice exam. If the learning outcomes correspond to higher levels of Bloom's taxonomy, assessments might need to be more complex, such as an essay, a presentation, or a group project.

Once the summative assessments are planned, online instructors then need to plan the formative assessments and learning activities that will help students prepare for the summative assessments. Sometimes this means scaffolding learning activities to allow students to master basic concepts they can work on at higher levels later. Finally, online instructors gather and create the learning resources students need, such as readings, multimedia content, and lectures.

While Bloom's taxonomy is the most common taxonomy used, other models of alignment can provide helpful guidance for effective course design and instruction. For example, educators who prefer a nonhierarchical

TABLE 1.3
Sample Alignment Chart Using Bloom's Taxonomy

Learning outcome	Cognitive domain	Summative assessments	Formative assessments and learning activities	Learning resources
Outcome 1: After successful completion of the course, students will be able to present a persuasive argument	Synthesis	Final persuasive essay	In-class activity identifying ethos, pathos, and logos appeals in advertisements; homework assignment analyzing persuasive appeals of several authors; first draft and peer review exercise for final paper	Assortment of advertisements using different persuasive appeals; published persuasive essays to use as models; rubric to guide peer-review activity
Outcome 2:				
Outcome 3:				

Note. Based on Bloom (1956).

multidimensional lens for classifying learning that might not be sufficiently represented in Bloom's cognitive domains may find Fink's (2003) significant learning model more applicable. Fink's model encourages educators to design learning experiences that help students establish foundational knowledge, the application of new skills, a human dimension where personal and social implications are considered, a caring dimension where students develop interest and values, and a metacognitive dimension where students learn about the process of learning. These dimensions are not hierarchical but are simply different perspectives through which to engage learners with topics of study. Educators who are more interested in the overall intellectual development of students may find more value in Perry's (1999) scheme, which views student learning through a lens of larger developmental stages. Instructional faculty use this scheme by adapting their interactions with students to the students' perceived developmental stages, steadily guiding them toward more mature and sophisticated ways of thinking and engaging with the discipline and world.

Regardless of the alignment model adopted, practicing alignment in designing an online course is like writing a paper with a strong thesis and a well-constructed outline as a guide. Using alignment models as a framework for course design can help to ensure consistency, intentionality, and thoroughness in a course rather than a haphazard or random assortment of lessons. They can help educators understand and communicate how various lessons in a course relate and work together. From the student perspective, strong alignment helps to create an online course that comes across as clear, cohesive, and purposeful, and which therefore may help students understand how they are learning what they are learning. From the educator perspective, choosing and using an alignment model can help you design and deliver courses according to your teaching values.

ADVANCE PREPARATION OF COURSE MATERIALS

Another core competency for online teaching is the ability to prepare course materials, in advance, that will offer sufficient and engaging guidance for online, asynchronous

INVITATION TO REFLECT: ALIGNMENT

1. See the sample alignment chart template in Table 1.3 and use it as a model for your own. In columns, list the following from your course for each learning outcome: the cognitive domain for each outcome in Bloom's (1956) taxonomy, the summative assessments, the formative assessments and learning activities for each outcome, and the learning resources needed.
2. In mapping your course's alignment, did you find any examples of misalignment? Do they correspond to parts of your course where students tend to get confused, wander off topic, or lose interest?
3. For any areas of misalignment, how might you adjust your course?

learners. Of course, all college instructors, regardless of the modality they are teaching in, must prepare course materials. Online instructors, however, because they will not have students gathered in one place at one time to answer questions, should take special care that documents such as assignment directions are concise, thorough, and clear and that these materials are engaging for students. Another reason that the preparation of course materials is a core competency for online educators is that there are simply more course materials to prepare for online courses than for face-to-face courses due to the absence of synchronous in-person meeting time.

For instructors teaching traditional, on-campus courses, course preparations might include writing the syllabus, creating a weekly schedule of topics and reading assignments, and forming an evaluation plan listing the major assessments for the class and how each is weighted. These preparations typically take place prior to the beginning of the course and, given the busy schedules of many instructors, usually immediately prior. Then, an instructor might plan each week's lectures, learning activities, and assignments a step or two ahead of each scheduled class meeting. This is often done so the instructor can be responsive to student learning needs throughout the term. In many ways, the course preparation and the actual teaching of the course are blended into one workflow and are not distinct activities.

With online teaching, however, course development and teaching are two distinct bodies of work, happening over two distinct periods of time because online course development requires significantly more writing than that needed for on-campus teaching. The increased amount of writing required necessitates a shift in workflow and requires development and teaching to be handled separately. The concurrent prep and teaching approach used on campus does not work well for online education, because the writing, and sometimes media development, require additional time and effort. If online educators tried to develop content just a few steps ahead of their students, they would quickly be outpaced and overwhelmed.

In addition to the syllabus, schedule, and evaluation plan, online educators must write far more of what they need to communicate to students in advance. Although on-campus instructors have the benefit of constant interaction with students during the compressed development and teaching phase, and they can use those interactions to determine whether they should spend more or less time covering certain topics, online educators must anticipate those interactions and prepare content in advance for a multitude of possibilities. When online educators prepare a solid core of content in advance, as well as a framework for interaction, they are able to devote more time during the semester to interacting with students.

Which materials should online educators be preparing? A well-designed, well-developed online class requires online educators to produce several categories of course materials:

Course Introductory Materials

- Course orientation, a welcoming overview of the course, an explanation of how the course is organized, what kinds of participation will be expected of students, and how to progress through the course materials

- Course syllabus, including all required university and instructor policies, plus a statement on online etiquette; information on communication expectations; directions about how to contact the instructor from a distance; the technical requirements for the class; and instructions on how to access technical support, library holdings, and student services from a distance
- Directions for any technologies, software, or online publisher-provided content and activities

Week or Unit Introductory Material

- Overviews that introduce the learning objectives; explain how they support the course learning outcomes; and preview the learning activities, assignments, and assessments for the week or unit of study
- Reading and resource lists, often with introductory comments that provide context and guidance for students about the significance of each resource or that alert students to pay close attention to certain aspects
- Written materials and visuals that deliver or support course content
- Written lectures, or transcripts for any recorded lecture content, as well as informative alt-tags, which are textual descriptions for any images meant

to convey instructional content so that students with disabilities can access the course materials when using adaptive technology for the visually impaired

- Visuals for any recorded lecture content, such as PowerPoint presentations, screencast recordings of the instructor working through problems or sketching graphs, and any diagrams or images the instructor needs to convey content
- Copyright permission requests or fair-use documentation for any content the instructor would like to borrow from other sources to include in the course materials on an ongoing basis

Directions for All Student Activities

- Directions for all learning activities, ideally including grading criteria and rubrics
- Discussion questions, carefully constructed to support and encourage meaningful dialogue, as well as follow-up questions the instructor saves for later to ensure full coverage of the discussion topic

Assessments

- Directions for major projects, papers, or assignments, often broken down into several steps to be staged over time
- Quizzes and exams, often including automated feedback, especially for formative assessments

Well-designed online classes are carefully constructed to use an architecture of engagement.

#ThriveOnline

Furthermore, in addition to being written in advance, these materials need to be built into the learning management system, with all the right settings, before the class begins. Clearly, the writing requirements for creating an online course are significant. Online educators who adopt a two-stage approach, first developing and then teaching the course, typically find they are able to enjoy both phases more, if only because they have time and energy to perform well in both phases.

Preparing online course materials is more than simply presenting content in a one-way flow of information. The preparation of course materials also includes setting up a framework for interaction. Well-designed online classes are carefully constructed to use an architecture of engagement. There are times when the instructor is putting out information, but there are also times when the instructor is guiding students through a critical thinking exercise and times when the instructor must provide some room and structure, but not too much, to create an environment where students will work together in a learning community to meet learning outcomes. This architecture of engagement needs to be written and built into the learning management system well before students are present in the class.

The empty shell in the learning management system is the classroom. It begins as a vast digital space with no discernable architecture. Online educators need to create that architecture so that students know how to move around and behave in the space once they arrive. If it were a physical classroom, not writing the course in advance would be akin to inviting students into a room

INVITATION TO REFLECT: ONLINE COURSE PREP

Have you ever developed an online course while you were teaching it? How does this experience compare to developing online courses in advance?

Invitation to Connect
Share your experience of developing an online course using #ThriveOnline.

---

before the building was even constructed. Preparing a traditional campus-based course takes time and planning, but preparing an online course requires much more. Preparing an online course is like building a (virtual) classroom and writing a short, interactive book.

ASYNCHRONOUS COMMUNICATION SKILLS

Communication skills are important for every educator. Online teaching, however, requires a specific kind of communication skill: the ability to communicate asynchronously, because the classroom is virtual and attendance is asynchronous. Some educators new to online education imagine an online course is everything an on-campus course is minus the face-to-face instruction. Experienced online educators know, however, that a well-designed and well-facilitated online course replaces face-to-face synchronous interaction with online asynchronous inter-action, and asynchronous interaction requires specialized communication skills. There are several specialized asyn-chronous communication skills, some of which are used in the design and development phase and some of which are used in the facilitation phase.

Technical Writing Skills

Technical writing, which is writing with a purpose of informing, explaining, or providing directions is a critical specialized communication skill for asynchronous instruc-tion. Much of the writing needed for online courses is necessarily technical in nature: weekly overviews, announcements, assignment and exam directions, feed-back on student work, written lectures, and discussion prompts and posts. These are all passages of writing that are meant to inform or to provoke certain behaviors from readers. Traditional on-campus educators provide much of this content verbally. Of course, they do need to write assignment directions and feedback, but they are able to converse with students informally to provide context and background information about the assignment and indi-cate which aspects are most important. Online instruction, however, has a far greater dependency on the written word, specifically on the technically written word that is meant to inform, explain, and provide direction.

Furthermore, the heart of technical writing is under-standing that the purpose is to inform and shape the behavior of the reader. Technical writers know they share the responsibility of making meaning with the reader.

They understand that the way they shape their writing has a direct impact on how readers will receive, understand, and respond to their messages. If technical writers do not do their jobs well, people who purchase products will be unable to use them and will be frustrated, or worse, injured. Imagine the results of poorly written instructions for performing maintenance on a lawn mower. Technical writers understand that they have a responsibility to create messages that work to get specific results for their readers. The technical writer does not have the luxury of saying, "If readers do not understand, it is their fault and their problem." The technical writer bears tremendous responsibility for readers' success, sometimes even for their safety and well-being.

Similarly, with the writing they do for online courses, online educators bear a tremendous responsibility for their students' success. Taking this responsibility is a big shift in thinking for some educators in higher education who believe they have studied and have become experts in their fields and that their role is to lecture about what they have learned and then test students on how much of that information they have absorbed. In that model, students bear the responsibility to make meaning—to listen, interpret, read, investigate, and learn the material in whatever ways they can. Shifting to a model that requires shared responsibility is a new way of thinking for some educators.

In an online classroom, and in online portions of hybrid courses, there is no front of the room where the instructor can stand and communicate information. There are no rows of seats where students file in and sit down.

The written word directs what happens, at least at the outset. Of course, in well-designed online courses, students will engage in active learning and will form learning communities, but usually it's the written word that first greets students in an online class, which sets the stage for the unscripted activity and communication that follow. Online educators who practice some basic principles of technical writing often report that they receive fewer questions about assignments and find students have less confusion about what is expected.

Fortunately for those who do not have strong technical writing skills, even a few basic writing techniques can help pave the way for successful interactions with students in asynchronous online courses as well as in online portions of hybrid courses. Once educators observe how well students respond to these writing techniques, how they help students get oriented to the course material or activity more quickly, and how they help educators connect with students more meaningfully, the techniques quickly become habit.

INVITATION TO REFLECT: YOUR WRITING SKILLS

1. Which kinds of writing do you have the most experience with?
2. Which kinds of writing are you most comfortable with?

Shaping the Message to be Comprehensible

Experienced online educators understand that comprehension is not solely the responsibility of the reader and that the writer must shape the message to be comprehendible. Applying some basic technical writing skills to online course materials helps bridge the distance gap. That is, good writing helps make up for the lack of opportunity to tell students in person what you *really* mean by the assignment instructions. In online asynchronous courses, instructors do not have all class members assembled at once. Therefore, they need to provide all the directions in one document, including the larger context, significance, and relevance.

Technical writers who create user manuals and product directions face the same challenge; their readers will need to rely on a written document to complete a task. If their readers are not able to make sense of the directions, they will contact the company with questions or complaints and possibly even return the items they purchased. Worse, they may injure themselves and file a lawsuit. For online educators, the stakes are different. Students will likely not be physically injured by poorly written assignment directions. However, there can be negative repercussions. If assignment directions are not clear, students may complain; drop the class; or, in extreme cases, petition for tuition refunds.

Statements of Purpose

One simple thing to add to an existing set of assignment directions to improve comprehension is a statement of purpose. With written directions, technical writers begin with a statement of purpose that allows readers to understand the objective or what they will accomplish if they follow the written directions. For example, directions that accompany a new chain saw might have two sets of directions, one beginning with "Follow these setup instructions before using your chain saw for the first time," and the other beginning with "Follow all directions to operate your chain saw safely." Readers can tell by the manufacturer's statement of purpose which set of directions they need, depending on whether they are setting up the tool for initial use or refreshing their memories prior to the annual pruning of backyard fruit trees. The statement of purpose tells users what reading the directions will help them do.

Similarly, online educators will use a statement of purpose at the beginning of an assignment or activity to tell students what reading the directions will help them do. In on-campus courses, educators have the opportunity of communicating the statement of purpose orally when they are handing out the assignment sheet or when they project the assignment on the overhead screen to introduce it. When online, though, educators do not have students assembled all at once, so they need to include that statement of purpose in the assignment directions. For example, the statement of purpose in an online course that introduces a term project might read like this: "This term project will help you explore a potential career path by analyzing educational requirements, typical career progression, occupational outlook, and ranges of salary rates in various geographic regions." Or, "This project will give

INVITATION TO REFLECT: STATEMENT OF PURPOSE

Open an assignment you use in one of your classes. Does it have a statement of purpose? If not, draft one. If it does, can you improve it by helping students connect to something they already know or by emphasizing how they will use the information or skills in the future?

you experience working with data sets, analyzing data, and communicating your findings using data visualization techniques—important skills in today's information-driven world." By providing a statement of purpose such as these, online educators provide a useful map that tells students where they are going and a preview of how they will get there. These statements of purpose can also help students connect the project at hand with what they already know and help them envision how they will use the learning experience in the future.

Formatting Matters

Formatting features are not just nice-to-have extras. They help convey meaning with visual rhetoric so that readers understand the nature of the idea being expressed before they even start reading.

Most of the people teaching in higher education had to do substantial amounts of academic writing to earn their advanced degrees. Those academic writing habits can be hard to break, especially when part of your job is to indoctrinate students in those same writing skills and habits. Online educators may come to realize that setting aside academic writing habits and borrowing techniques from technical writing can help online students understand information as well as follow directions successfully. Writing styles suitable for these purposes include formatting features that help students preview information, scanning ahead to see where the passage is going, and then returning to the start to digest details. Headings, subheadings, and guiding questions such as those found in frequently asked questions sections or lists help students preview the big picture and then immerse themselves more fully in smaller details.

Using bulleted lists to break down an idea into categories or components helps students process information more quickly for a couple of important reasons. First, the bulleted-list structure encourages concise writing. Second, the list structure itself helps readers understand at a glance that the idea being expressed is a larger category with several different parts. Lists help readers understand the structure of the idea quickly, which then prepares readers' minds for the details. Numbered lists do the same but are especially helpful in situations where readers may need to go back and forth between the directions and the task at hand. Numbered lists are preferable to bulleted lists in these situations because they help readers quickly pick up where they left off by quickly finding the number in the list instead of having to search the list for the applicable bullet.

Educators accustomed to academic writing may be more comfortable at first with explaining an assignment or learning activity in lengthy paragraph format, but using formatting features such as the ones described here brings more white space into the document, thus grouping ideas in more digestible chunks. Use Box 1.2 to help develop your technical writing skills.

Box 1.2 Technical Writing Checklist for Online Educators

- Have you started each set of directions with a statement of purpose?
- When providing step-by-step directions, have you used numbered lists instead of paragraphs?
- When longer passages are necessary, have you used headings, bulleted lists, or other simple formatting features to convey the structure of an idea even before the idea itself is read?
- Have you broken your expository text or assignment directions into smaller chunks?
- Have you used white space to visually separate smaller chunks?
- Have you written concisely?

A FEW WORDS ABOUT WRITING CONCISELY

Those who are well practiced in academic writing are accustomed to a writing style that is detailed, thorough, exploratory, and sometimes even expansive. Online educators need to curb those instincts when writing directions and informative passages for their online classes by trimming unnecessary words, avoiding redundancy, and eschewing passive voice in favor of active. Less is more in writing for online courses. Perhaps ironically, writing concisely can take more time and effort. This investment in the development period of creating an online class, in taking extra care with your writing and in other preparatory activities, pays dividends once the teaching begins, as students will feel less confused and more confident about your ability to guide the class. You will also spend less time answering student questions if directions and course materials are clear.

USABILITY AND MOTIVATION

In addition to technical writing, another asynchronous communication skill and competency needed for online teaching is an understanding of usability. *Usability* is a term used in software engineering to describe how easily and efficiently people using the software are able to complete the tasks they need to complete. Poor usability means that people struggle to find what they need or do not understand how the software functions. Good usability means that people are able to efficiently complete tasks seamlessly, without struggle and without the assistance of help documentation. To achieve a high degree of usability, software engineers need to understand people's expectations, assumptions, and motivations so that they can create an experience that works with them instead of against them. From the consumer standpoint, a high degree of usability means that people find the experience satisfying and effective and are more likely to choose that product over others.

In the context of online education, usability means understanding how students move through and behave in an online space and how these behaviors differ from other educational environments. In the face-to-face classroom, students take seats facing the front of the room and wait for the educator to lead the day's lecture, activity, or discussion. The instructor leads and the students follow. And, when the instructor distributes written assignment directions or an article to read, we know students will read from left to right and top to bottom. In both the physical classroom and in the written assignment, the educator/writer drives, presenting the sequence of ideas, and the reader follows, along for the ride.

Online, however, the reader is in the driver's seat. Hyperlinks and clickable navigation mean that the reader has many options and the power to exercise them. In an online class, this means students have the ability to move from one area of the course to another. Indeed, to force students to go through a particular sequence in a learning management system is difficult. You have to adjust many settings and create interdependencies, which creates more risk that the course will malfunction. Newer learning management systems are designed to give students navigational choices; it is more difficult now to restrict those choices because they are often included in the default design.

This means that online educators writing course materials and building online courses need to work with those navigational choices instead of against them. They need to understand the various paths students will take through the materials and design them to make sense, regardless of the path students take. At least to a small degree, online educators have to think like software engineers and try to understand student expectations, assumptions, and motivations that inform their behaviors in the online setting. Some students will navigate to weekly learning modules in a course and work through content and activities in sequence, but others will jump around according to their interests. Some students will navigate from a calendar or to-do list in the learning management system—some of which aggregate due dates for all the courses a student is enrolled in. (Consider the importance of standardized naming conventions in such a system: Homework 1 or Discussion Post versus Math 111 Problems or Philosophy 300 Discussion Response.) Frustratingly for some instructors, many students focus on graded activities and begin with assignments, discussions, and quizzes, going back to the course content only on an as-needed basis to fill in gaps.

Indeed, one of the most challenging aspects of online education is that students tend to focus on the course components that have points assigned to them. In traditional campus-based classes, instructors can somewhat rely on social norms and positive peer pressure to motivate students to complete readings and to participate in nongraded learning activities. Not participating in a face-to-face discussion or activity or coming to class routinely unprepared would be uncomfortable and awkward. Even in on-campus courses where some students are unprepared, usually the class can count on a few motivated students to carry the discussion so everyone can move forward.

Motivation plays a significant role in education regardless of modality, but online educators will find that motivation is deeply connected to usability in the online setting. Students in any learning environment learn better when they find educational content intrinsically motivating, that is, enjoyable in some way. Success rates also increase when students find learning activities extrinsically motivating and when external factors can be internalized and integrated (Ryan & Deci, 2000). For example, an external motivator that is internalized and integrated is when students see a future benefit for their education or career. On campus, most students find nongraded classroom-based learning activities enjoyable and intrinsically motivating because they are interacting with peers. Or, they are extrinsically motivated by pleasing a watchful instructor. Online courses offer more anonymity for these nongraded activities, and the asynchronous nature of online courses means that students are often in the classroom alone. As a result, motivating online students to use the online course content in the manner the educator intends can be more challenging and can require specialized approaches.

Like traditional campus-based instructors, online educators need to make an effort to motivate students, either intrinsically because the activities or resources are inherently enjoyable or interesting, because they are extrinsically motivating in that there is a future educational or professional benefit for students, or by attaching points to these activities. However, online educators may need to build motivation more intentionally and strategically into the course. Including a link to an inherently enjoyable video in a course is not sufficient; the link needs to be contextualized and presented as enticing in some way. This might mean crafting some introductory text that introduces a learning resource to pique curiosity or emphasize a future benefit to make studying the resource more clearly motivating. This might mean designing a resource or learning activity relating to the resource that will be graded for the online environment, even when the same activity would not necessarily be a graded component of an on-campus version of the course.

These are all concerns that online educators should take into account because student behavior differs somewhat in on-campus and online learning environments. Some instructors I have worked with who are first learning about online education have balked at suggestions to assign points differently for their online courses, as if students needed to be spoon-fed the course content. However, I suggest that this approach is simply a question of usability and designing the course materials in a manner that is suited for the environment. Usability in an online setting is part clarity and navigational ease but is also part motivational strategy.

EXPLORING USABILITY IN YOUR ONLINE HABITS

For those teaching online, there is value to being well-practiced users of the Internet, especially interactive portions of the Internet such as online forums, social media, or commerce sites where social interaction plays a role. The best way to design something well is to first be an aficionado of what you are trying to design. If you are

Motivation is deeply connected to usability in the online setting.

#ThriveOnline

INVITATION TO REFLECT: STRETCHING YOUR USABILITY SKILLS

Outside your teaching responsibilities, how do you interact with others online? In which ways do you read or view the contributions of others? In which situations do you contribute? For example, do you read online reviews before making a purchase? Have you ever written a review? Why did you use your valuable time in this way? How would you describe your motivations for doing so?

1. Experiment with social media. If you already use some social media tools, try a new one. For instance, if you are already using Facebook, try opening a Twitter account. Explore Instagram, Snapchat, and Reddit. How do communities of users form in each of these social media outlets? How do the people know, or not know, each other? How do they organize themselves? Which rules of engagement do you observe in each?

2. Consider your students' engagement in these online communities. What kinds of expectations might they have for engagement in an online class? As you explore, note whether there are forms of engagement you find appropriate for an online class or if there are any you believe may be inappropriate.

writing novels, you should read many classic and contemporary titles. If you are creating music, you should listen to a lot of music in your genre and related genres. And if you are creating an online course, it is helpful to be familiar with how and why people typically interact with each other online.

Invitation to Connect

Which forums or styles of engagement might be useful if adopted or adapted for online learning in the classes you teach? Share your ideas on social media using #ThriveOnline.

CONTENT DELIVERY SKILLS

Another important competency for many online courses is the ability to deliver content in a way that meets usability needs and expectations for today's online students. Initially, the technical aspects required can feel the most daunting. Simply selecting and learning to use the right software may seem like a challenge. Indeed, online lectures can take a variety of different formats. The following are some potential options:

- Slide deck voice-overs where instructors begin with PowerPoint as the visual component (using software such as Adobe Presenter, a PowerPoint add-on, or screen-capture software such as Jing or Screencast-O-Matic)

- Tablet-created visuals such as sketching graphs or working through equations with voice-over (using software such as Camtasia or Captivate)
- Videography, ranging from a studio-recorded sequence in front of a green screen, with backgrounds added in postproduction or professionally shot in the lab or field, to low-tech instructor-recorded videos with a laptop webcam
- Podcasts or audio recordings, if visuals are not necessary

Selecting from these options can feel overwhelming. To simplify the choice of software, it can be helpful to identify the visuals the instructor wishes to use and make the selection based on that aspect. If there are existing slides or a need to demonstrate software, a voice-over-screen option would be the best choice. If the instructor needs to work through an equation and explain a sequence of steps, using a tablet with voice-over recording would be effective. Of course, identifying the software and hardware options available at your institution is also an important part of the decision. Even if your institution is not well equipped, many free and low-cost options are available. With a simple microphone and free online tool such as Screencast-O-Matic, educators can create simple but effective learning materials.

In addition to choosing the right technologies, the question of *how much* content should be presented is an important one. It is not uncommon for educators moving from a lecture-based, on-campus style of teaching to assume that delivering the same content when teaching online requires recording three 45-minute lectures for each week of class because that is what they did on campus. In online courses, however, long lectures broadcast for students with no interactivity are not effective. In thousands of conversations across the country, instructional designers tell educators who are making a transition from teaching on campus to online that online lectures should be significantly shorter than those delivered on campus. In response, they hear complaints, decrying the waning attention spans of students today.

Hibbert (2014) found that the average view time of online videos is only about four minutes. However, she cautions that video content in online courses varies considerably in terms of purpose and production value, and we should be careful not to deduce from the average four-minute view times that all instructional videos must be less than four minutes in length. Hibbert's (2014) study found that higher view rates occurred when video content was well integrated with direct connections to course assignments and assessments, such as videos that provided overviews of important assignments when graded course components were based on video content and when the video presented material that written passages could not convey, such as "timing, body language, vocal delivery, etc." (para. 14). Additionally, instructor presence (especially when humorous), production value, and students' metacognition about their own viewing habits affected how well and how long students used course video content (Hibbert, 2014).

Similarly, in a study of interactivity and instructional scaffolding on learning in online video-based environments, Delen, Liew, and Willson (2014) found that features such as "note-taking, supplemental resources, and practice questions . . . enhance learning by making the environment more interactive" (p. 319). Furthermore, they found that students who used video with interactive components "invest or spend more time in the learning process, resulting in enhanced or superior learning outcomes" (Delen et al., 2014, p. 319). The U.S. Department of Education (2010) did find that online students may perform marginally better because they are spending more time on task.

Indeed, if we look at today's students in other areas of life, we do not see waning attention spans. More students in this generation than in previous ones are attending school and working to support themselves at the same time. Carnevale, Smith, Melton, and Price (2015) present the following statistics:

> About 40 percent of undergraduates and 76 percent of graduate students work at least 30 hours a week. About 25 percent of all working learners are simultaneously employed full-time and enrolled in college full-time. Adding to their stress, about 19 percent of all working learners have children. (p. 11)

Working and attending school at the same time means prolonging periods of concentration throughout each day, not decreasing attention.

When considered in this context, today's online learners may not have attention span problems. Thus, perhaps the problem with delivering long lectures in an online format is not about a lack of attention but about

Long lectures do not suit expectations for the online medium.

#ThriveOnline

usability. Perhaps the problem is that long lectures do not suit expectations for the online medium where students expect to self-direct their activities and interact with content, the instructor, and other students.

Although we know that a 45-minute, 1-way, noninteractive broadcast video is not effective for online learners, there is no magic video length that will be effective in online courses. However, by applying the following strategies, some for shaping video messages and others for shaping student behavior, video lectures can be better integrated into online classes to encourage students to spend more time on task, thus encouraging better learning outcomes.

Shaping Your Content

- Establish your presence, especially with humor.
- Share what you found difficult about something you are teaching students.
- Share, discuss, and disprove common misconceptions about the content you are presenting.
- Make comparisons with things students already know.
- Ask students to make predictions about what happens next.
- Tell stories, which encourages readers to remain longer to find out how the story ends.
- Pause every so often to say what you mean when presenting facts or data.
- Find or create professionally produced, visually appealing video content when possible for important or complex content.

Shaping Student Behaviors

- Provide direct instruction about expectations for student viewing habits while viewing online course video content, such as note-taking, reflection, and discussion about the content.
- Identify which video content is required versus which is optional.
- Call student attention to specific segments of relevance for longer videos.
- Associate graded course elements, such as assignments or graded discussions, with required video content.
- Build interactive components into video and lecture content, such as asking comprehension questions, taking notes, or requiring students to create video responses.

Other Ways of Providing Course Content

Although lecturing is certainly one way to provide course content, there are many other ways to present content for online students. Reading materials including textbooks, journal articles, and Internet resources will be part of virtually all courses. In addition, some institutions offer professional multimedia development in which online educators may be able to enlist professional support to create content in other formats, such as the following:

- 3D animations that show how something moves, grows, or mechanically operates

- 3D scans of specimens or objects that students can rotate to see all sides and zoom in for close-up examinations
- 360-degree photography or videography that allows students to explore and study a location
- Virtual reality that allows students to step into simulated environments such as distant rain forests, different periods of history, or labs
- Augmented reality that allows students to view 3D images using their smartphones or tablets

Even at institutions that are not able to offer the support of professional multimedia developers, there are still many engaging and effective methods of presenting content other than lecturing that instructors can find ready-made or create independently, such as the following:

- Documentary films, which are often available online, through university libraries, and on popular streaming services such as Netflix
- Infographics, which can be found online or easily created with free online tools (many even have templates available for those who are not artistically inclined)
- Time lines, found online or created with free online tools
- Curated content from the Internet such as interviews with experts, recorded demonstrations and experiments, podcasts, TED talks, or other open educational resources

- Content created with rapidly advancing smartphone technology, such as 360-degree photography and 3D scanning

In addition, instructors in some disciplines and courses find it effective to have students research and present content to each other. This approach requires careful synthesis and moderation by the online educator but can be an effective means of encouraging students to interact with and learn the course content.

Whether you need to lecture to present content in your course depends on a variety of factors, such as your discipline, the texts available for your topic, or the level of the course you are teaching. In many cases, instructors who used the lecture method of teaching in on-campus courses find they are able to teach the same courses successfully online without lecturing or by lecturing very little in comparison. Devout lecturers moving to online teaching may have a difficult time accepting this. It is challenging to give up a comfortable method of teaching or to learn to do things in new ways, but there are advantages for online students in doing so.

Educator Identity

Some traditional campus-based educators do not cling to the 45-minute lecture because of mere habit. Some seem to feel that if they are not lecturing for extended periods of time, they are not doing their jobs and are not meeting their students' needs and expectations. Ultimately, this is a question of identity and how you see yourself and your role as an instructor.

INVITATION TO REFLECT: DOES YOUR ONLINE COURSE NEED LECTURES?

1. Are you teaching a foundational course for a degree program in which students need to master terminology, basic concepts, or facts they will later work with in different and more complex ways?
2. Are most of your course learning outcomes at the lower two cognitive domain levels of Bloom's (1956) taxonomy: knowledge and comprehension?

If you answer yes to both questions, your course may need at least some lecture content. However, if you can answer yes to the next questions, you may want to consider reducing or eliminating lectures entirely from your course design.

1. Do your planned lectures simply echo information students are already reading in a textbook? Which rules of engagement do you observe in each?
2. Can your students learn what you are trying to teach by participating in an activity rather than from a lecture?
3. Are most of your learning outcomes at higher levels of Bloom's (1956) taxonomy of cognitive domains, such as application, analysis, synthesis, or evaluation?
4. Can students do research and then create something based on what they find to demonstrate their learning, such as with a presentation, speech, or Web page?

ASYNCHRONOUS DISCUSSION FACILITATION SKILLS

Finally, and perhaps most importantly, the competency most educators must master to be successful in teaching online involves designing, facilitating, and grading online asynchronous discussions.

Traditional on-campus instructors know there is an art to leading face-to-face class discussions, asking the right questions, and knowing when to interject and when to hold back and let interactions among students play their course. Timing class discussions in synchronous class meetings can be challenging. Many instructors teaching multiple sections of the same course notice that different groups of students will take different lengths of time to talk through course topics. As a result, instructors must plan conversation accelerators for the slow groups and conversation expanders for those who get through material quickly. Instructors must also be able to sense when a group of students needs to pause for synthesis and reflection. They must know how to engage the reticent students at the back of the room and temper the enthusiastic participation of those at the front without dampening their enthusiasm. Sometimes, just when the conversation is getting to something meaty in a synchronous class, the scheduled period is over and students must disperse.

Interestingly, instructors who excel at leading face-to-face discussions can struggle in making the transition to facilitating online discussions. Common complaints from instructors new to the online environment are that

INVITATION TO REFLECT: HOW DO YOU SEE YOUR ROLE AS AN EDUCATOR?

1. Fill in the following blanks to explore how you perceive the role of an educator. As you complete this exercise, you may wish to include details from formal or informal education experiences.

Recalling your past learning experiences with educators:

   a. The best instructor I ever had was ___, because ___.
   b. The best learning experience I ever had was ___, because ___.
   c. The last time I needed to learn something new, I ___.

Identifying perceived expectations:

   a. In my teaching, my students expect me to ___.
   b. My colleagues expect me to ___.
   c. My department expects me to ___.
   d. My university expects me to ___.

Exploring your view of yourself as an educator:

   a. When they leave my course or program, I want my students to be able to ___.
   b. As an instructor, I feel the most joy when ___, because ___.
   c. My best teaching moment was when ___.

2. Now read through your answers. How do the educators portrayed in each section compare? Perhaps more interestingly, how do they contrast?
3. Which components do you want to emphasize in your own teaching moving forward? Which will best serve students in your courses? Which perceptions might you be able to relinquish?
4. Finally, how do these reflections about your role as an educator affect how you think about delivering content for online students?

discussions can seem repetitive, feel overly formal as well as too informal, appear shallow in terms of student engagement with the subject, and that students complain that they feel like they are doing busy work.

One response might be to impose policies to try to address these issues, but sometimes these policies can be convoluted or misguided. For example, some instructors might require students to research all their posts and include formal citations. Some adjust the learning management system settings so that students must contribute their first post in a vacuum, that is, before reading other student contributions to the same discussion. Others impose strict word count minimums or maximums. Still others require every single student to provide an outside resource with each post. Perhaps the most misguided of all are instructors who absent themselves from the online class discussion forums because, they say, those are spaces for student interaction and that their presence there as an instructor impedes authentic discussion.

Imagine the havoc that could be wreaked if we inflicted these kinds of class discussion policies in face-to-face courses. Imagine an on-campus class discussion requiring the following:

- Every contribution requires a written source and must include a quotation or paraphrase and bibliographic information.
- Students must line up in the hallway and enter the class one by one to respond to a question. After everyone answers, the instructor plays a recording of all student answers to the same question—for everyone to hear.
- Students respond in their own words, but they must count the words. If they express their idea but fall short of the word count, they must keep speaking anyway. The instructor tallies the word count and assigns grades accordingly.
- Instructors announce they will no longer attend class discussions because discussions are for students. Their professorial participation in class discussions only stifles conversation. For the rest of the term, if students have questions, they should send the instructor an e-mail.

When we imagine these ill-conceived online discussion policies in the face-to-face setting, their flaws become more apparent and even comical.

Perhaps the most pervasive misguided policy of all, though, is what I call the line-up-and-answer model, which requires all students to address the initial question posed by the instructor in a discussion post and then return later in the week to reply to the posts of two peers. On the surface, this kind of participation policy seems to make sense. It seeks to encourage interaction between the student and the content and among students and their classmates. There is also room for the instructor to follow up, which allows at least the possibility of interaction between the students and the instructor. Fostering these three forms of interaction is a good approach. However, in seeking to build in sufficient interaction, instructors requiring this participation scheme seem to have failed to realize what the experience of the ensuing discussion would be.

Imagining this same policy applied in a face-to-face discussion can help illustrate the essential flaws of this model. Imagine a face-to-face classroom where the instructor asks one question and then the students all line up to answer the same question. After the first four or five students respond, answers quickly become repetitive, and the remaining students begin to feel as though they have nothing of value to contribute. Their feelings are justified, for what could possibly be the point of all that repetition? The discussion does not stop there, though. After every student has given the answer to one question, each is then required to reply to two other students.

Is it any wonder discussions designed like this fall short when compared to face-to-face class discussions? Truly, if we imagine any of these misguided discussion policies applied in a face-to-face classroom, we quickly see that the instructors imposing these policies seem to have forgotten that online discussions are first and foremost *conversations*. Instructors who have tried using these policies and practices often conclude that the fault is in the medium and that online discussions will just never be able to match face-to-face discussions in depth, breadth, or quality. However, with the right approaches, online asynchronous discussions can not only equal the depth, breadth, and quality of on-campus discussions but also, indeed, exceed them.

DISCUSSION PURPOSES

A strategy in leading online asynchronous discussions is to determine the purpose of your planned discussion. The previous misguided policy suggests that the purpose of an online asynchronous discussion is to assess student learning. However, asking all students to answer the same question and then grading the correctness of each response is not a discussion but rather a quiz, and a poorly administered one at that, because students are able to hear each other's answers.

Stepping back to observe a discussion or to describe a discussion from memory can help us notice key attributes that signal the purpose and value of the conversations. Review your answers to the questions in the following Invitation to Reflect, then consider a few of your answers in more detail.

INVITATION TO REFLECT: DISCUSSION PURPOSES

Recall a face-to-face class discussion you have participated in either as an educator or as a student. Or, ask a colleague if you may sit in on a face-to-face class discussion to observe. Then answer the following questions:

1. How did the discussion begin? Did the instructor present a brief lecture or pose a question to the class?
2. Did all students participate or only some? When did they participate? Was it voluntary or compulsory?
3. Did the conversation include any disagreements? If so, describe them in some detail. Who were the parties in disagreement? Were the parties in disagreement individuals or groups of individuals? How did the instructor participate in this portion of the discussion?
4. Did the conversation include any tangents? Did the instructor at any time try to halt one part of the conversation in favor of pursuing another aspect of the topic?
5. How were resources incorporated into the discussion? Were students expected to prepare in any way? How did they demonstrate (or fail to demonstrate) preparedness?
6. Did the instructor offer any summary, synthesis, or take-away messages during or at the end of the conversation?
7. What value do you believe students found in being present for the conversation?

Stepping back to observe a discussion or to describe a discussion from memory can help us notice key attributes that signal the purpose and value of the conversations. Review your answers to the questions just asked, then consider the following:

1. What conclusions can you draw from what you observed about the purpose of this discussion?
2. Can you recall or imagine other discussions that may have alternative purposes?

As you may have discovered in the "Discussion Purposes" reflection activity, more than one purpose is possible for class discussions. A model for productive online discussions by Gao, Zhang, and Franklin (2013) suggests that four purposes, or dispositions, are possible: comprehend, critique, construct knowledge, or share. Discussions with a purpose of building comprehension require students to actively engage with content to demonstrate their understanding, listen to relevant details others mention, and make connections. Discussions with a purpose of critiquing involve argumentation, which can lead to students questioning their prior assumptions. Discussions with a purpose of constructing knowledge involve students stating varying personal interpretations and understandings and improving their own knowledge as a result of these social interactions. Finally, discussions with a purpose of sharing involve students participating in a learning community having a sense of responsibility for each other.

Online discussions can not only equal the depth, breadth, and quality of on-campus discussions but also, indeed, exceed them.

#ThriveOnline

Online discussion forums can also be used for purposes other than conversation (Riggs & Linder, 2016). Other purposes for online class discussions might be for presentation space, where students make formal presentations and respond to questions; a gallery and reflection space, where students create, share, and interpret images related to the discussion topic; or as a work space where students collaborate on group projects, exchange and discuss peer reviews, or work with partners on a math problem or debugging a computer code.

A NEW MODEL FOR ONLINE DISCUSSIONS

Perhaps ironically, because of the pervasiveness of the line-up-and-answer model discussed earlier, students in online courses need to be reintroduced to the normal habits of class discussion with which they are familiar from face-to-face contexts. That is, the instructor will launch the class discussion with a comment or question. Then, a few students will participate, addressing the instructor and perhaps each other. Another student may interject with a question, which might then be addressed by a fellow student or the instructor. As the discussion progresses, the instructor may refocus the group or advance the discussion by posing follow-up questions. In other words, online students may need to be reminded that online asynchronous discussions can operate in the same way as traditional face-to-face conversations.

PARTICIPATION SCHEDULES FOR STUDENTS

For a more natural conversation practice to work in the online asynchronous environment, it is helpful to establish participation schedules. Given what we know about busy schedules of online students, especially those who are seeking their entire degrees online, it makes sense that most of these students would prefer to complete the majority of their coursework on the weekends. Because of the asynchronous nature of online discussions, however, allowing students to participate only or mostly on weekends diminishes the quality of the discussion because it limits the number of interactions between students and the instructor and among students themselves. Requiring students to participate throughout the week ensures that conversations will have breadth and depth and that more natural conversations will take place in the online environment.

PARTICIPATION SCHEDULES FOR ONLINE EDUCATORS

Likewise, online educators' participation throughout the week is also important for ensuring the breadth, depth, and naturalness of the conversation. Everson (2009) identified several categories of online instructor discussion participation: confirming students are "on the right track" (para. 5), calling attention to important points of discussion, posing follow-up questions for students to clarify or extend their thinking, correcting misunderstandings, and providing "direct instruction" (para. 5) when students get significantly off track. Considering the nature of these categories of instructor contribution, the importance of the timeliness of the instructor's response becomes apparent. If students are off track, for instance, and the instructor is absent from the conversation for a number of days, students may misinterpret the lack of intervention as confirmation that the off-track posts are actually correct. As a result, for the best facilitation of online discussions, online educators should plan to participate in discussions multiple days per week.

The ways that the instructor participates on the occasions when students need clarification and at the ends of units of study are also important for student success. When instructors correct mistakes in whole-class online discussions, the tone used in making corrections should be clear and direct yet should also avoid shaming or condemning individual or groups of students. Providing clear and correct information to students is important for their learning; however, maintaining high levels of motivation to keep students engaged is also important and must be considered in balance. Instructors often post summaries of key points at the ends of online discussions, which are important, but they can ask students to identify key points as well.

GRADING ONLINE DISCUSSIONS

Earlier in this section, the model of online discussions as assessments was challenged. Online discussions are much richer when they are approached as conversations, not as assessments. However, this does not mean that online educators should not grade discussions. At first this may seem paradoxical; however, the meaning becomes clear when we consider more carefully what exactly is being assessed when we grade online asynchronous discussions.

The earlier critique of approaching online discussions as assessments involved assessing the correctness and accuracy of individual student responses to a single question or set of questions in a public forum. If an instructor wishes to assess individual student comprehension of specific questions, a quiz or homework assignment conducted privately is a much better tool for meeting this goal.

So, in grading online discussions, if we are not to assess correctness, what should the grading criteria be? The direction here will vary depending on the purpose, the nature of the online discussion or activity happening in the discussion space, and a number of other variables; however, the following criteria may be considered as examples for alternatives to assessing in the line-up-and-answer model of online asynchronous discussions:

- Participation over a required number of days per week
- Engagement with the topic, as shown by references to class reading materials and other resources, authentic questions and applications, and original interpretations
- Appropriateness of contributions, such as referencing reliable sources, demonstrating sound logic, and demonstrating habits of mind appropriate for the given discipline

INVITATION TO REFLECT: DESIGNING A BETTER ONLINE DISCUSSION

Select an online discussion from a course you teach that has not been as productive as you desired and may benefit from revision.

1. Consider the four discussion dispositions Gao and colleagues (2013) present, which are comprehend, critique, construct knowledge, or share. If you consider your course learning objectives, in relation to your discussion topic, which disposition or purpose is the best fit?

2. Consider other discussion formats, such as those from Riggs and Linder (2016): making presentations, sharing and discussing images, or participating in small-group collaborations. How might you use one of these activities in relation to the topic you wish students to discuss?

3. What are the current participation requirements for students in your online courses? What are your participation habits? How might these be adjusted to promote improved conversations?

4. Which practices, habits of mind, or other traits specific to your discipline do you want students modeling in your online discussions? How can you model or encourage them in your class discussions?

5. Which criteria have you used in grading your online course discussions in the past? Are there any modifications that might make sense with this grading approach?

The question of how much to weight discussions in the overall evaluation plan for the course will also depend on the discipline, level of the course, purpose of the discussions, and so on. However, online educators should try to make discussions weighted enough to encourage participation by all students and in proportion to other assessments in the course.

SIDE CONVERSATIONS: AN INTERESTING ADVANTAGE

In face-to-face classes, sometimes side conversations can break out, and when they do, they are generally considered rude and are discouraged. Sometimes, though, the side conversations can be a lot more interesting than the main conversation thread, perhaps because there is a need for differentiation for a given subset of the class or perhaps simply because students are making an interesting and unforeseen connection.

In online discussions, when side conversations break out, they can and often should be encouraged. The asynchronous nature of the conversation means that several threads of discussion can be happening simultaneously without disrupting the whole group, and participants are free to pursue them all in their own time. When online, it is not rude to jump into those side conversations because the asynchronous nature of the conversation means you are not interrupting anyone. As a result, online, the final conversation is not only a chronological or linear, logical narrative but also a rather complex web of communication with many interesting branches and tributaries. Furthermore, in this conversation, if the instructor has designed and facilitated it well, every student has participated meaningfully, not just the few eager beavers at the front of the room.

SELF-ASSESSMENT

Several preparations, skills and core competencies for online educators have been presented and discussed in Part One of this book: training for online educators, including aspects of course design and facilitation; alignment as it pertains to online course design; specific writing skills that help online educators communicate more effectively; understanding of and attention to usability concerns in course design; and asynchronous discussion skills needed to ensure high-quality, in-depth interactions for learners. As you seek to thrive in your career as an online educator, a thorough self-analysis of your skills and expertise is an important first step in building confidence and determining where you may need additional professional development or support.

Once you have completed a thorough self-assessment of your preparedness, skills, and abilities related to online course design and teaching, you likely will have discovered many reasons to be confident in your role as an online educator. Ariel Anbar, director of the Arizona State University Center for Education Through eXploration, characterizes the challenges associated with teaching online

INVITATION TO REFLECT:
ONLINE TEACHING SKILLS

Take a few moments to reflect on the skills and expertise you use in your teaching. Here are 10 prompts to help you uncover and identify the skills and expertise you may have that will contribute positively to your experience teaching online.

1. Describe your technical abilities and computer skills. Which programs do you routinely use? How often do you experiment with emerging technologies?
2. Rate your troubleshooting abilities. Which strategies and resources do you use when you encounter a technical difficulty?
3. Describe your writing skills. Are you able to communicate in writing clearly and concisely? Are you able to write persuasively?
4. Are you organized? Are you someone who prepares in advance and avoids procrastination?
5. Do you have a feel for usability? Can you vividly imagine how students will interact with the course materials you create? Are you able to anticipate problem areas and where students may become confused?
6. Do you enjoy or have experience using social media to communicate with friends, family, or colleagues?
7. Have you experienced for yourself an engaging asynchronous discussion or exchange of ideas?
8. Have you pursued any professional development or training about online course development or teaching?

9. Have you taken an online course or participated in a massive open online course? Do you know what it feels like to be an online student?
10. Have you explored other instructors' online courses or course materials?

in the following: "Be aware that it is still not as easy to teach well online as it is to teach poorly online, and that is still harder than teaching poorly in person" (A. Anbar, personal communication, June 4, 2017). Indeed, online teaching requires significant preparation, skill development, and expertise, including online-specific training, understanding of alignment and application of it in course design, specialized communication skills, knowledge of usability and motivation of online students, content delivery skills beyond the classroom lecture, and asynchronous discussion design and facilitation skills. While these competencies may seem daunting if you are just starting out, it is important to recognize that the important thing is to begin. Many educators, perhaps yourself included, began traditional classroom teaching careers feeling uncertain and lacking in confidence but over time have developed skills and confidence that helped them feel at ease in that environment. Learning to teach in the online environment works the same way. With experience, reflection, and some professional development, you can feel as confident and energized in the online space as you do in other environments.

Recognizing that millions of students each year are calling on educators to deliver high-quality learning experiences online can also help motivate you. There is a high demand for online education, and it is growing. So many aspects of online teaching are compelling and inspiring. Some online instructors are drawn to the prospect of reaching learners worldwide. Others find that online teaching balances well with family life. Another reason to seek online teaching opportunities is that good teaching is good teaching, regardless of the modality, and the rewards of teaching can be found online and are not restricted to a specific physical location behind a classroom door. Many find great energy and pleasure in teaching students who attend class when they are ready to be there and when they can be rested, attentive, and focused, not because competition for classroom space necessitated 8:00 a.m. meeting times. Finally, educators new to online teaching, when they design and facilitate their courses well, delight in discovering that online teaching is as much a human endeavor as face-to-face teaching. Online courses do not consist of computers talking to computers but of people using technology to connect with other people in the pursuit of knowledge. Once we move beyond the question of *whether* online education can be done well to *how* it can be done well, suddenly we find ourselves on new ground—fertile ground in which educators and their students can thrive.

KEY TAKEAWAYS FROM PART ONE

- Results from studies of online education's actual efficacy and perceptions of online education's efficacy indicate a gap between actual learning outcomes and faculty/administrator beliefs about learning outcomes in online education.

- To thrive in online teaching, it is helpful to shift the conversation from *whether* online teaching can be done well to *how* it can be done well.
- Face-to-face and online learning environments share some fundamental common ground but have some key differences.
- Many key teaching proficiencies are necessary in both environments, but online teaching requires some unique teaching skills and competencies.

TAKE ACTION TO THRIVE

Whether you are new to online teaching hoping to learn the basics, an experienced online educator hoping to mature and grow in your teaching, or an administrator seeking to support online teaching and learning at your institutions, there are actions you can take to reach a thriving state in your career.

For Educators New to Online Teaching

- Complete a self-assessment of your online teaching knowledge and skills.
- Identify your strengths. How are you already thriving online?
- Where might you need some additional professional development to improve your sense of thriving? Where can you get this professional development?

For Online Educators Seeking to Grow

- Review your use of discussion forums. What is the purpose of each discussion? Does the design of your discussion prompts help students achieve that purpose?
- Check the alignment of your course components using a taxonomy that is meaningful for you, such as Bloom's (1956), Fink's (2003), Perry's (1999), or another. What adjustments can you make to infuse your teaching values more fully into your course design and teaching?

For Administrators

- Do online educators at your institution receive training specific for online course development and facilitation? What training resources do you have at your institution? Which might need some cultivation?
- Are workloads organized to allow for discrete development and teaching phases? How might your institution be able to accommodate the time and work quality online teaching and learning require?
- Describe perceptions of online education at your institution. What opportunities do you have to shift the conversation from *whether* online teaching can be done well to *how* it can be done well?

PART TWO

THRIVING AS AN ONLINE EDUCATOR

THRIVING AS AN
ONLINE EDUCATOR

Changing the conversation about online education from the question of *whether* online education can be done well to *how* it can be done well can improve the overall experience of the course for the students and can lead to greater professional satisfaction for the instructor. This shift in the way we talk about online education signifies a meaningful shift professionally as well. By asking *how* instead of *if*, we signal our commitment, intention, and determination to succeed. The title of this book and series isn't *Determined to Succeed Online*, though; it is *Thrive Online*. So, while intention is important, how can we move beyond intention and determination to achieve a state of thriving? What does it mean to thrive in the day-to-day work of being an online educator?

Before we can answer this for ourselves in the context of our careers, it can be helpful to step back and consider what we mean, exactly, by thriving more generally. Spreitzer, Sutcliffe, Dutton, Sonenshein, and Grant (2005) define *thriving* as "the psychological state in which individuals experience both a sense of vitality and a sense of learning at work" (p. 538). The sense of aliveness and the sense of developing knowledge and skills must be present to count as thriving because we can feel alive and energetic without learning, and we can learn while feeling worn out. Spreitzer and colleagues (2005) contrast thriving with feeling depleted and as though we are languishing. When thriving, we are working hard, learning, moving forward in some way, and we feel energized and motivated by our efforts. Thriving includes two aspects, one emotional and one cognitive.

In addition to identifying the two necessary components of thriving, the affective feeling of vitality and the cognitive advances in learning, Spreitzer and colleagues (2005) identified three specific behaviors that help generate the sense of thriving in the work environment: task focus, exploration, and heedful relating. Each of these behaviors promotes feelings of vitality and learning:

- Task focus, the experience of being absorbed by our work, makes us feel alive and energized. When it leads to task completion, we feel even more satisfied because of our achievement. Task focus also contributes to learning because we are actively paying attention and because, usually, when we

Thriving includes two aspects, one emotional and one cognitive.

#ThriveOnline

accomplish tasks routinely, we are permitted to be more autonomous in our work, which adults find motivating and conducive to learning.

- Exploration, or experiences and information that are novel, brings feelings of vitality because new discoveries tend to engage our interest and are therefore energizing. With new experiences, exploration also brings plenty of opportunity for learning.
- Heedful relating is when people "act in ways that demonstrate that they understand how their own jobs fit with the jobs of others to accomplish the goals of the system" (Spreitzer et al., 2005, p. 541). This behavior brings about feelings of aliveness through a sense of belonging and social connections with others, which in turn provides opportunities to learn with and from others.

Each of these behaviors can be counted on to bring about necessary components of thriving, including a sense of aliveness and intellectual development. As educators seeking daily practices that can help us thrive in our professions, this framework provides us with a useful lens. The following discussions elaborate on Spreitzer and colleagues' (2005) concepts of task focus, exploration, and heedful relating in the context of the day-to-day work of online educators. Each discussion is followed by questions to help you develop concrete daily practices and behaviors to help you intentionally cultivate your sense of thriving in your online teaching career.

TASK FOCUS FOR ONLINE EDUCATORS

At a foundational level, as in any work environment, task focus for online educators includes ensuring that we get enough rest and exercise and that we follow a nutritious diet. Although this advice may seem obvious, consider how many of us working in higher education get by on too little sleep, rarely make time to get up from our desks to go for a walk, and substitute coffee shop snacks for wholesome meals. Those of us working in online higher education may fare worse because we spend too many hours hunched over a computer, not even pausing to walk from our offices to class and back again. For too many of us, reaching for the shift button on the keyboard is the biggest stretch of the day.

In many higher education work cultures, we wear these unhealthy habits like badges of honor, almost bragging about working long hours and drinking too much coffee. These unhealthy behaviors then spread because the implication is that if we do not overwork and under-care for ourselves, we are not as hardworking or dedicated as those who do. However, just the opposite is true. We should take care of ourselves because doing so is good for us *and* because doing so will make us better at our jobs. If we want to improve our focus and mindfulness, we need to treat our brain as if it were part of our body. Daily practices online educators can perform are getting enough rest, exercise, and nutritious food. Task focus is simply not possible when there are long-term deficits in any of these areas.

Interestingly, there are many types of apps you can download on your phone, tablet, or computer to remind you to take stretch and movement breaks from your electronics. Several even provide guidance for exercises to reduce eye strain. By taking time to take care of our health, we ensure we are at our physical and mental best when we are at work.

Invitation to Connect

As an online educator, how do you practice self-care? Please share using #ThriveOnline.

Task Focus: Prioritizing Important Work, Including Online Teaching Work

Another factor contributing to task focus is prioritizing our work. Establishing and maintaining a regular schedule is one way to ensure time for work-life balance, but it can also help to ensure we allot sufficient time and prioritize tasks that should be taken care of during working hours. Again, maintaining a regular schedule for work tasks may seem like obvious advice, but consider how many hours we spend on tasks that impersonate priorities in our work days: responding to an e-mail immediately as it comes in, allowing it to interrupt what might have been focus time; answering cold calls from sales personnel; online window shopping, news reading, cat video watching, or other Internet distractions; allowing the office chatterbox to monopolize our time; or accepting invitations to meetings we do not really need to attend. Interlopers on our task focus time will vary, but if we take some time at the start of each term and even at the start of each week to prioritize what we want to accomplish and hold time on our calendars for those true priorities, we can minimize the tasks that use our time for no real benefit.

For educators who are teaching in multiple modalities in online, hybrid or blended, and face-to-face courses, this prioritization should account for balancing the needs of online students equally with those of traditional campus-based students, as well as with other face-to-face demands such as department and committee meetings. It can be tempting to prioritize face-to-face demands such as a student knocking on your office door or meeting requests from colleagues over a student waiting to connect with you digitally. It is easier to ignore students who are geographically remote and visually hidden behind our screens. However, if we shift our priorities to favor the face-to-face demands on our time too often, our online teaching will suffer. Or, we will suffer when we end up using time that should be dedicated to rest or exercise to catch up with online teaching work. Stealing important recovery time is not good approach to task focus. If we truly want to thrive as online educators, we need to prioritize the time we spend conducting online teaching tasks. Online educators who are seeking to thrive should schedule dedicated time daily for online teaching. Block out online teaching time on your calendar as through you were going to be in the lecture hall.

Another way educators may unknowingly not prioritize online teaching is by being underprepared because of a lack of training, a lack of advance course development, or a lack of usability testing for newly adopted educational technology. When we are underprepared, courses do not run as smoothly, and we must devote what should have been task focus time to cleanup activities, problem-solving, and clarifications. An important daily practice for online educators is to work well ahead of our students, such as developing future semester courses in advance, making time for training and professional development, and testing all links, technologies, and course materials before our students access them.

Task Focus: Creating Routines to Build Efficiency

The adage "practice makes perfect" is certainly a familiar one, but practice with task focus creates a sense of thriving. Spreitzer and colleagues (2005) said, "When individuals focus on their tasks, they are more likely to develop and refine routines and repertoires for doing their work efficiently and effectively" (p. 541). The efficiency and effectiveness brought about with repetition and practice yield feelings of increasing competence, vitality, and learning—in other words, thriving.

Finding routines that work for online teaching is important in helping find efficiencies and improving effectiveness for students and for ensuring enough focused task time for online teaching. Of course, every class is different, and there will be significant differences depending on disciplines, levels being taught, and instructors' styles and preferences. You may need to try several approaches to establish routines and repertoires that will work for you. The following discussion provides some aspects of

For educators teaching online and on campus, the needs of online students should be prioritized equally with those of on-campus students.

#ThriveOnline

online teaching to consider as you discover your own optimal routines and repertoires.

Online Asynchronous Discussion Pacing

The pacing of online asynchronous discussions can be difficult to master but doing so is well worth the effort. In a well-designed online course, the discussion forum is often the heart of the class and is where most of the interaction and learning happen. Getting the discussion boards moving to the right rhythm can make all the difference. That rhythm is created with frequency of participation—not the overall number of posts, but rather the number of days per week or unit that require student participation. Participation requirements for students help set the pace.

Everson (2009) argued that the instructor's role in online discussions is very important in ensuring student satisfaction with online courses. Many educators find it beneficial to be present in the discussions even more often than students, not necessarily for long durations but with greater frequency to keep up with the flow of conversation. In synchronous discussions, hundreds of back-and-forth interactions can take place during a one-hour meeting. Because everyone is not present at once when online, each hour of participation must be spread out over multiple days to reach the same number of interactions and the same depth and breadth of coverage.

Term-Length View of Educator Discussion Participation

Faculty participation in weekly discussion forums is important, but it is more important at the start of the term.

Many experienced faculty find their participation in online discussions needs to be greater early in the term but can safely drop off a little in the middle of the term or beyond. This is because the educator has set expectations and has established presence and trust with students. Once that foundation is set, students feel comfortable playing a larger role.

Online Educator Workflow

Educators also need to pace their visible presence in an online course with presence that is less visible but just as important, such as for grading and providing feedback in a timely fashion. Figure 2.1 provides an example of how an online educator might distribute the workload for one online course during a week. The rhythm for your class may vary considerably, but planning how to spend the time you have each week for your online course can help you prioritize and improve task focus. This figure shows that this example instructor devotes more time to grading and feedback on Monday and Tuesday, with more class discussion time Wednesday through Friday, and a significant amount of prep time for the coming week also on Friday. Online students tend to be working adults. As a result, they tend to complete substantial amounts of coursework on the weekends. Figure 2.1 shows a standard Monday-to-Friday work week; however, you may find it effective to shift some work time to the weekends at least to check in to see if there are urgent questions. Some learning management systems allow educators to receive text message alerts when students post in a particular forum; making use of these kinds of settings can reduce your weekend workload.

Figure 2.1. Sample time management.

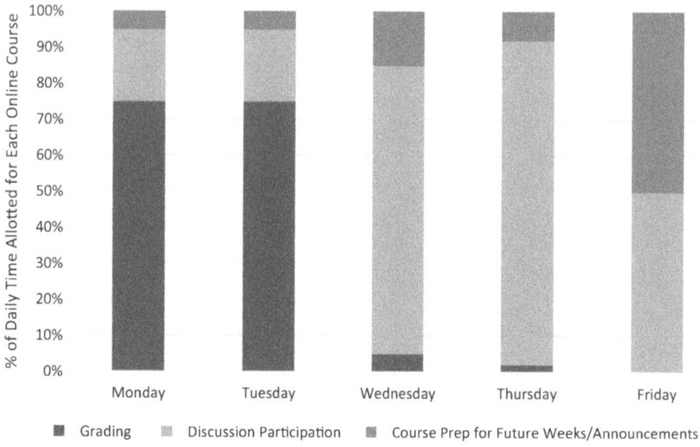
% of Daily Time Allotted for Each Online Course
100%
90%
80%
70%
60%
50%
40%
30%
20%
10%
0%
Monday
Tuesday
Wednesday
Thursday
Friday
Grading
Discussion Participation
Course Prep for Future Weeks/Announcements

Balancing Student and Instructor Workloads

Two different workloads, the instructor's and each student's, must be paced manageably so they do not conflict. As you plan your course calendar, consider which times are heaviest in terms of workload for you and for your students. Balance the two workloads so that during weeks you are busy providing robust feedback on a large number of papers or projects, students have an activity they can handle somewhat independently. Likewise, when students are busy drafting and revising those papers and projects, you can use that time to do some longer term teaching work, such as developing or redeveloping online content for future terms.

To thrive, we must have feelings of vitality and aliveness, as well as feelings of learning or advancing in our work in some way. Knowing how much time we have

INVITATION TO REFLECT:
TASK FOCUS FOR ONLINE EDUCATORS

1. Fold a piece of paper lengthwise to create three columns.

   a. In the first column, list five tasks related to teaching that make you feel most energized and alive.
   b. In the second column, list five aspects of your teaching that students seem to appreciate and value most.
   c. In the third column, list five tasks related to teaching that drain your energy, fill you with dread, or that you routinely put off for another time.

2. Examine your lists and consider what your teaching priorities have been and how they might be able to evolve.

   a. Are there synergies where an energizing task for you is also an aspect of your teaching that students value?
   b. Are there tasks you routinely perform that deplete your energy and that students do not seem to appreciate or need?
   c. Are there ways you can modify the energy-depleting tasks to minimize them or make them less draining?

Recognize that finding the right balances will take some trial and error. Keep at it until you strike the balance that works for you.

available to devote to each class we are teaching and prioritizing the teaching responsibilities that have the greatest impact are important steps in achieving task focus for online educators. When we make time for what is important, we create an environment that fosters a strong task focus. And when we accomplish this, we feel alive in our work and are able to thrive.

The reflection questions in the "Invitation to Reflect" box on the previous page will help you reflect on your teaching responsibilities and priorities, as well as on how you spend your teaching time. Are you engaged enough in task-focused behaviors?

EXPLORATION FOR ONLINE EDUCATORS

In addition to task focus, the behavior of exploring yields a sense of thriving. Making time for exploration can be especially challenging for those of us working in higher education, however, because exploration is not explicitly necessary in the way that tasks such as grading student work, responding to e-mails, and answering student questions are. As a result, we often relegate exploratory activities for when we have time, which is rare to never, even though we recognize that such activities enable us to learn and energize us in our work.

Perhaps the most obvious way to explore as online educators is by attending conferences about online teaching and learning. These immersive exploratory experiences offer immense value as time away from routine tasks can be devoted entirely to exploring new ideas and meeting new people. Sadly, even when we can find the resources and time to attend conferences, we are often so overwhelmed with catch-up work when we return that it can be easy to set aside all we have learned and fail to put it into practice. To help ensure you put new conference explorations to good use, consider some of the following strategies.

Before the Conference

- Identify your learning goals and plan your session attendance accordingly. What are you most interested in exploring? Be sure to stray outside your comfort zone for at least one or two sessions to extend your learning.
- Review the speaker biographies and check your social media networks to see if there are colleagues you would like to meet at the conference. Arrange to meet for a meal or at a conference break in advance. Some of the best conference explorations happen between sessions in those informal conversations when we find out what colleagues at other institutions are doing.

At the Conference

- Resist the urge to multitask while attending conference sessions. Just because you can check e-mail during a session does not mean you should. Why travel to a conference to do work you could have done more efficiently and comfortably in your office? Use your e-mail system's out-of-office message response to let students and colleagues know you are spending time away to focus on improving your teaching.

- At conferences, you will be overwhelmed with new and useful information. Taking notes is essential, and you can make more of your notes by sharing them with a larger community. Use a blog, Twitter, or another form of social media to record your most salient notes. Use conference hashtags to network digitally with fellow attendees. Laura Pasquini, facilitator of the Online Learning Consortium's Developing Your Social Media and Digital Presence for Higher Ed Staff workshop, lists several benefits of these communications:

  > Today's backchannels offer a way to showcase professional development opportunities, disseminate scholarly research, distribute resources for practice, curate knowledge from an event, and archive the learning so that it "lives" beyond a geographic location, calendar date, and so on. (L. Pasquini, personal communication, June 25, 2017)

- Keep a running list of action items to complete after the conference, such as e-mailing a speaker to request more information about a presentation, reading an article or a study mentioned in a session, trying out a new educational technology you learned about, or implementing a new teaching practice.

After the Conference (Retain and Use What You Learned!)

- Block a couple of hours on your calendar within a week of your return from the conference. Use this time to pull your notes together, sort literature you gathered, and send follow-up correspondence. Plan how to put your action items into practice.
- Share something you learned at the conference with a colleague or group of colleagues once you return home.

If your budget or schedule does not allow conference travel, there are other ways of exploring that are more affordable and easier to fit into busy schedules. Some conferences provide the option of Web access for certain sessions, so if you are not able to travel, you can sometimes remotely attend a live conference session. Free or fee-based webinars can also be affordable and schedule-friendly exploration opportunities. Massive open online courses are another great way to explore. Education-related blogs and podcasts are an excellent way to feed your professional development needs if you can dedicate time to them on a regular basis.

Exploration: Off the Beaten Path

Sometimes the most fruitful explorations are not quite so research intensive or goal driven. Exploring unexpected and even unrelated places can lead us to thrive. Julia Cameron's (2002) international bestseller and creativity movement, *The Artist's Way,* is partly founded in a

INVITATION TO REFLECT: EXPLORING RESOURCES FOR ONLINE LEARNING

1. What were the most useful conferences about teaching and learning you have attended?
2. What were the most useful professional development opportunities at your home institution?
3. What education-related blogs and podcasts do you find inspiring and informative?

Invitation to Connect
Share your favorite resources on social media using #ThriveOnline.

non-goal-driven practice called "artist's dates" (p. 18). The workplace-related adaptation by Bryan, Cameron, and Allen (1998) is also partly founded on the regular practice of non-goal-driven explorations, which in this version are called "time-outs" (p. 24). The objective of artist's dates and time-outs is to make time for play and to absorb new experiences and information. In practicing them, participants devote an hour or two of alone time each week to a fun or new experience, such as visiting a museum or gallery, touring a botanical garden, shopping for art supplies, or simply taking a walk.

Creating an online course is, or at least *can* be, a creative act.

#ThriveOnline

The weekly solo outings during the 12-week creativity-boosting programs outlined in these books are assigned for reasons other than rest or pleasure:

> Creative work draws on an inner reservoir that we must consciously restore and replenish. . . . If you put images and energy out, you need to put images and energy back in. This is not goofing off; it is tuning in to your own creative needs. (Bryan et al., 1998, p. 24)

The principle here is similar to the one by Spreitzer and colleagues (2005): "Exploration makes it possible for employees to encounter novel ideas, information, and strategies for doing work; this exposure to novelty can provide and restore energy" (p. 541). In the professional context of online education, artist dates or time-outs can be time well spent for educators seeking to increase their feelings of vitality and learning. Creating an online course is, or at least *can be*, a creative act.

Peruse the following examples to see if any might work for you.

Exploring the Internet and the online medium itself can be a worthwhile regular if not daily practice for online educators. The Internet, social media, and educational technology change rapidly, and with these changes our interactions change as well. Isolating ourselves in stagnant online courses will mean our course designs and our inter-actions with them can quickly grow stale.

The Internet is a multimedia jungle, teeming with life and growing exponentially every day. Many online courses unfortunately do not reflect this richness. To explore, online educators can commit to making the most of the online medium by bringing media in all forms to the class. Instead of trying to replicate the on-campus learning experience, we should be trying to create the best possible learning environment the online medium allows. Online courses provide a rich multimedia experience for students, which is one thing that online courses are better at than traditional brick-and-mortar learning environments.

Online educators can enrich their use of the online medium and practice the thrive-inducing behavior of exploring by regularly scouring the Internet for multimedia resources to use in their courses. Video resources abound and can easily be found through outlets such as YouTube, Vimeo, and TED.com. Further exploration can allow instructors to vary the types of media they use by including images, animations, simulations, games, and audio recordings. These components can improve student learning engagement in courses in several ways, for example, by adding novelty, gaining student attention, and provoking students to consider course topics from fresh perspectives.

As you gather new media artifacts, however, curate carefully. So many resources are available that it can be tempting to include too many. Be critical. Include only the best resources you can find and be sure to remove stale media content as you bring in your new discoveries. Remember, too, that most media objects need to be woven into the course content and learning activities to encourage students to use them. If we simply drop media objects into the course with no introduction, context, or guidance for interaction, students will quickly think of them as window dressing and not something they are meant to use.

Your exploration of the online medium might also expand beyond course content and resource hunting to include investigating new forms of social media. Beyond fresh content, explorations into these kinds of applications have less to do with content and more to do with the ways people interact online. Consider how people used to use print newspapers. Most read the paper and maybe discussed what they read with family and friends. A few wrote letters to the editor. However, interaction with online news sources is significantly different now. Online readers have a much more active role, as news we read online is easily shared with our networks. Readers also comment publicly far more frequently than they ever did when their only option was to write and mail a letter to the editor; the medium has made it easier to express their opinion.

Likewise, our social media tools make it easy for people to interact, but all social media tools are not alike. Each new tool has its own nuances, strengths, and weaknesses and brings with it different kinds of interactions that change and keep changing the way people communicate and learn. As online educators, we can regularly explore how people interact in these new digital spaces and monitor emerging kinds of interactions for those that can be useful in online teaching.

Table 2.1 provides a high-level overview of several well-known social media applications, including how people tend to interact on each platform and each platform's

TABLE 2.1

Social Media Characteristics, Strengths, and Weaknesses for Online Learning

Application	Interaction characteristics	Strengths	Weaknesses
Blog	Topic based; allows sharing text, images, videos, and links to other content; users tend to find content by following specific blogs; users interact by commenting on blog posts and by linking to other blogs	Allows deep topic coverage; can be visually engaging	Can be difficult to attract readers and to find blog content that is not attached to a known media outlet
Facebook	Profile based; allows sharing text, images, videos, live streaming, and links to other content; users see content shared by friends and pages they follow; users communicate by indicating if they like the content and by providing comments	Widely adopted; stable audiences can be created and maintained; allows creation of closed groups	Tends to be reserved for personal use; privacy settings are complex and can restrict ability to share; has been criticized for returning results based on the user's point of view rather than an accurate reflection of multiple or opposing viewpoints and for minimizing conflicting viewpoints

(*Continues*)

Table 2.1 (Continued)

Application	Interaction characteristics	Strengths	Weaknesses
Instagram	Image based; relies primarily on the use of hashtags to gain viewers; users communicate by indicating if they like the content and by providing comments	Visually engaging; allows open sharing	Sharing of ideas tends to be shallow; presentation is more gallery like, without opportunity for significant discussion
LinkedIn	Résumé based; allows sharing text, images, and links to other content; users communicate by indicating if they like the content in groups and by direct messages	Professional in focus; allows creation of closed groups	Much of the content is promotional; spam can be a problem
Pinterest	Image based; allows sharing of text, images, and links to other content; users can follow each other or search for content by keyword	Visually engaging, useful for curating related content	Tends to be reserved for hobby-related use

Reddit	Text based; allows sharing of multimedia content and links to other content; users find content by browsing topics; users can signal approval with an upvote, resulting in more users seeing content with greater numbers of upvotes	Organized by topic; current news and information items move to the top; communities are formed around interest areas	Visually text heavy; can be challenging to navigate, especially to older content
Twitter	Text centric; allows messages with 140-character limit; allows sharing images, GIF files, and links to other content; users find content by following other users, browsing trends, and searching hashtags and keywords	Brief and often pithy; allows linking to lengthier content; identifies trending topics; allows replies and lengthy conversations, public and private	Challenging to organize content; can be time-consuming to navigate to older content

relative strengths and weaknesses in the context of the kinds of communication necessary in educational contexts.

Many social media outlets are available, but being active in all of them would be counterproductive:

> Be selective as to *where* you want to be online. You do not need to occupy all social media accounts; it is *not* possible. Pick and choose a few to "try on" and think about how these platforms connect with your own goals for getting started. Make a decision to leave it, if it is no longer relevant or it does not provide value to you and your intended outcomes for using it in the first place. Additionally, pick and choose *when* you go onto these platforms. It is easy to be consumed or distracted; however, you can negotiate when and where you will engage and interact online. You do not need to *always* be "on" social media to be considered an active contributor to your personal learning network. (L. Pasquini, personal communication, June 25, 2017)

Defining objectives for your social media use can be a helpful way to begin. Possible objectives might be promoting your work, collaborating with colleagues, disseminating or gathering knowledge, or simply improving your understanding about how people communicate online for educational purposes.

Exploring Pedagogy

Although exploring is typically external, some of the most valuable explorations involve oneself. Online educators

INVITATION TO REFLECT:
EXPLORING SOCIAL MEDIA

1. Create an account for a social media tool you are not familiar with. Choose a topic related to the subject you teach or perhaps related to online teaching itself. Explore the community and engage in conversation. Keep at it until you have a feel for the unique communication rhythm of the platform.

2. What do you notice about the types and styles of messages shared with this tool? Are there strategies or techniques you could borrow to shape content for your online class? For example, Pinterest allows curating images with annotations. Perhaps you could gather a collection of images with annotations to present course content to your students?

3. Evaluate the social media tool for potential use in your online class. Could it be useful for discovering new content to share? Could it be useful for student explorations, presentations, or communications? Could it be useful for you in connecting with other online educators in your discipline?

4. Having trouble getting started? Visit socialmediafor education.org and work through a simple survey about your teaching to obtain recommendations for specific social media tools and guidelines for their use.

seeking to thrive should do a thorough inventory of their own epistemological and pedagogical beliefs and practices to ensure they are in alignment, and they should occasionally review those beliefs and practices to monitor for changes and to ensure alignment remains consistent in day-to-day teaching methods. Table 2.2 provides a high-level overview of several theoretical perspectives on teaching and learning.

Certainly, more can be said about each of these perspectives, and several others exist and are worthwhile to explore. You may wish to extend this table in your journal to include other perspectives, which when applied well can be effective. The goal in exploring these theoretical perspectives is not to determine which one is best, but rather to explore which one is best for you as an educator and for the students in your classes.

For some educators, the overview in Table 2.2 may be new information. Many working in higher education are highly trained experts in their disciplines but have never actually been exposed to theories and practices of teaching and learning. As a result, we often teach the way we were taught, not realizing that other options and approaches are possible. In the face-to-face classroom, teaching the way we were taught can work, although many do question the efficacy of the lecture-exam model that has been traditionally so well regarded.

Interestingly, it is important to recognize that many of those teaching in higher education today were never taught in the online classroom. Teaching how they were taught is therefore not an option. As a result, forays into online teaching expose the deficit of knowledge about

Those teaching today were never taught in an online classroom. Teaching how they were taught is therefore not an option.

#ThriveOnline

TABLE 2.2
Theoretical Perspectives on Teaching and Learning

Theoretical perspective	Learning happens when . . .	Teaching happens by . . .	Examples
Behaviorism	Information is received, repeated as needed, and predictable behaviors happen as a result	Repeating information; providing practice and reinforcement	Educator gives a video demonstration showing how to solve a math problem, provides practice problems, and provides guidance and feedback based on student performance
Cognitivism	Students are provided with information they can later recall	Helping students make sense of complex information and helping them organize that information in their memories so that it can be recalled	Educator breaks down a complex topic into small digestible pieces; strives to gain student attention to make information memorable; elicits and assesses student ability to recall information such as on an exam

Social constructivism	Students do not receive knowledge; they build it in learning activities with others	Guiding problem-solving; helping students think through complex issues such as by asking questions that provoke reflection	Educator provides case studies presented to groups that must work together to develop a solution or response to the case presented
Connectivism	Students can navigate networks of information, resources, and people to work on real-world problems, often culminating in the production of artifacts	Introducing students to networks of information, resources, and people; guiding the creation of artifacts	Educator introduces a topic or real-world problem, requiring students to propose a project that addresses it; provides feedback or peer review opportunities; asks students to create a presentation or portfolio outlining the problem and proposing a solution

teaching and learning even more so than initial teaching efforts in traditional teaching environments. We do not have a model to follow, whether with intention or more subconsciously. To design and teach online courses well, we must have a clear theoretical perspective from which to begin.

Understanding the theoretical perspective you subscribe to as an online educator is important for several other reasons as well. Each theoretical perspective suggests an underlying view of what knowledge is, how student learning should be assessed, and which roles and responsibilities are important for the educator to fulfill. By understanding your theoretical perspective, you will be better able to design your courses. Perhaps more important, you will be able to ensure alignment among the various components of your perspective as misalignment can lead to student confusion, frustration, and ineffective assessment practices. For example, if an educator believes learning is a matter of navigating networks to solve real-world problems yet assesses students with a quiz based on required textbook readings, the class is likely to feel unfocused.

Too often we teach based on habit or on the ways we were taught. Practicing the behavior of exploration inwardly with reflection about our pedagogical perspectives can help us discover and correct discrepancies in our course designs and teaching practices. When we align our course designs according to our theoretical perspectives, our teaching will be clearer and more purposeful, and we are more likely to feel that sense of vitality as we teach.

The questions in the Theoretical Perspective reflection box will help you with your own inward exploration and will guide you through your own inventory of what you believe about the nature of knowledge, how people learn, and the proper role of the educator in the online classroom. This inner exploration will help you learn more about yourself and, it is hoped, will help you gain insights into the ways your current teaching practices align with your theoretical perspective. If you discover instances of misalignment, you can then make adjustments to compensate. As you make these discoveries, and as you clarify and improve your teaching practices, recognize that this is what it means to thrive.

INVITATION TO REFLECT:
YOUR THEORETICAL PERSPECTIVE

1. Consider your discipline and the ways you have learned in it. From Table 2.2, or based on other pedagogical knowledge you have, determine which theoretical perspective you believe is dominant in your field. (Note that this may not be your perspective, and that is okay.)
2. Next, consider your own learning experiences and list three you had when you believe you were learning and learning well.
   a. For each experience, what was the nature of the knowledge you learned? Facts? Skills you could demonstrate? The ability to solve a problem? Something else?

    b. For each experience, how did you demonstrate your learning either to an educator or to yourself?

    c. For each experience, how would you describe the educator's role?

    d. What can you deduce from your own learning experiences regarding your theoretical perspective?

3. To which theoretical perspective do you now think you subscribe? (Note that if you teach very different courses, such as an introductory survey course and a graduate-level project course, you may need to subscribe to more than one. As long as you are clear in your mind about what constitutes knowledge, how to determine if students are learning, and your role as an educator in each, subscribing to more than one perspective is okay.)

    a. In a course you teach, what do you believe constitutes knowledge?

    b. How can you tell when students are learning?

    c. What assessments are you currently using? From the theoretical perspective you have been exploring, do any other assessment possibilities come to mind?

    d. Which roles and responsibilities must you fulfill as an educator?

HEEDFUL RELATING FOR ONLINE EDUCATORS

In addition to task focus and exploration, the third and final behavior identified by Spreitzer and colleagues

(2005) that professionals can elect to perform to bring on feelings of thriving intentionally is heedful relating. Heedful relating is more than just connecting with others; it is connecting with others for a recognized and collective purpose to achieve a common goal. Online educators are part of at least three professional communities to which they can heedfully relate: a class community with students, the institutional community, and a community beyond the institution. Interestingly, we may spend a lot of time relating within these different communities, but the degree to which we are heedful in our relations varies. Too often, we may be downright unaware and inattentive.

Students, the Community in Our Classes

The first community we can heedfully relate to is our students, with the collective purpose of achieving course learning outcomes. However, if the learning outcomes abide only in the syllabus and fail to make an appearance anywhere else in the class, perhaps the relating is not as heedful as it could be. Too often in teaching this is the case. The outcomes are included in the syllabus as if they were some sort of required legalese, and then the instruction that follows focuses on each unit's topic, or each major assignment. Those details are important, but by divorcing the daily work of the course from the learning outcomes, we make it harder for students to understand how the details all fit together, and they can miss the big picture.

The first step for online educators is to design courses so that the assessments, learning activities, and resources align with course learning outcomes rather than following the table of contents in the accompanying textbook or by leading students from one major assignment to the next. The second step for online educators is to bring the discussion of the outcomes out of the syllabus and into the teaching of the course to help students understand the connection between daily activities and the over-arching course learning outcomes. When we design our courses this way, and when we use the learning outcomes throughout the course rather than in just the syllabus, we are heedfully relating. Instead of merely slogging our way through course content and assignments, we will be making progress toward larger goals, stretching our intellectual abilities as we continually seek ways to make these connections apparent to students in our many interactions with them. In other words, we will feel vital and energized; we are learning, advancing, and thriving.

Our Institutional Community

The second community we might heedfully relate to is composed of members of our institutions, with the collective purpose being the achievement of our institution's strategic goals and initiatives. Depending on our affiliation with our institution, however, we may not even be aware of these strategic goals and initiatives for a variety of reasons. Like a poorly designed course where the learning outcomes reside only in the syllabus, many institutions publish strategic goals on the university website but then fail to help the educators they employ connect with those goals in ways they can truly be accomplished.

Institutions of higher learning are especially notorious for failing to communicate their larger goals and purposes with part-time educators and non-tenure-track instructors. These educators are frequently hired shortly before the start of a new semester and are rushed through various human resources bureaucratic processes, often with barely enough time to prepare the course for students. Although tenured and tenure-track educators have more exposure to strategic goals and initiatives, they are often so overburdened they can find it difficult to make time to fully engage at this level. However, regardless of your professorial rank, there is value in heedfully relating at the institutional strategic goal and initiative level. By becoming aware of your institution's goals and initiatives, you can better understand how your work can offer support and contribute to these larger goals. Although we are all involved in teaching students, consider the different goals and initiatives that would be part of these different kinds of institutions of higher learning: public land-grant universities, private Ivy League universities, institutions focused on research, private institutions with religious affiliations, liberal arts colleges, community colleges, or institutions that serve single genders or specific underrepresented populations. Even though we are all engaged in teaching and learning, the larger purposes of each institution type can have a significant impact on what happens in our classes.

By investigating your institution's goals and initiatives, you can also often discover resources that support your teaching goals and that can help you and your students stretch intellectually. By taking part in these larger systems at a higher level, you may feel camaraderie with fellow educators rather than experiencing your work siloed in an individual classroom, whether you teach on campus or online.

#ThriveOnline Community

Finally, the third community we might heedfully relate to are those beyond our institutions who are teaching in online learning environments, the members of the #ThriveOnline network. In this professional group, our collective purposes are to advance the development of online teaching as a profession, to improve teaching and learning throughout higher education, and to discover how our relatively new digital connectedness is changing the ways people interact and learn. These are exciting and worthwhile goals, but too often we do not make the time to connect with others in this larger community, sometimes because we simply do not know how.

We are fortunate that the very impetus for higher education's evolution—information-related technology—also provides us with greater means to share what we know and discover, to form communities to analyze the challenging problem of the changing role of educators, and to find and create solutions. The questions in the "Heedful Relating" reflection box will help you reflect on the opportunities available for you to relate heedfully with others in your career. When you devote time to connect your daily tasks to larger purposes and contexts, you can imbue your work with a greater sense of purposefulness and vitality, and you will have more opportunities to learn from other professionals. Although you may be expending more energy in making these connections, thriving means you will not feel depleted but rather more energized as a result of your efforts.

INVITATION TO REFLECT: HEEDFUL RELATING

1. Aside from your syllabus, where in your courses might you discuss course learning outcomes? You might emphasize learning outcomes in your class on weekly introduction pages; as context for discussion questions; as context for links to external content; in assignment or lab directions; in exam study guides; and in presentations of course content such as lectures, tutorials, and other interactive media.

2. Develop an activity, discussion question, or low-stakes assignment asking students to interact directly with your course learning outcomes. The following suggestions can help get you started:

   a. Instead of a typical introduction discussion, ask students to introduce themselves and share one thing they already know about one of the learning outcomes in your class, plus one thing they would like to find out.

   b. Ask students to create a meme that cleverly communicates something related to a course learning outcome.

   c. As an end-of-course wrap-up activity, ask students to rank the course learning outcomes, justifying their rankings by discussing their significance in terms of their studies, development, and professional goals.

d. Which other activity, discussion question, or low-stakes assignment can you think of to help students be more cognizant of your course learning outcomes?

3. Visit your institution's website and locate its mission statement, strategic goals, and major educational initiatives. How does your course support these goals? How might it do so better?

4. Contact your institution's distance learning department, center for innovation, center for teaching and learning, or any department at your campus responsible for the professional development of faculty. Inquire about major pedagogical initiatives, student success initiatives, or other institution-wide efforts to improve teaching and learning. From which of these might you benefit?

5. Finally, using your preferred social media outlets, search for keywords and hashtags related to teaching in your discipline, teaching with technology, and online teaching. Share a resource, a lesson learned, or ask a question. Heedfully interact with your fellow online educators so you can #ThriveOnline.

THRIVING DURING PERIODS OF CHANGE

Learning to teach online involves change for every educator who decides to undertake this professional path. Interestingly, many believe that larger, even more significant changes within higher education are taking place. Adams Becker and colleagues (2018) see the fundamental role of instructional faculty as being in a state of flux:

> Educators are increasingly expected to employ a variety of technology-based tools, such as digital learning resources and courseware, and engage in online discussions and collaborative authoring. Further, they are tasked with leveraging active learning methodologies like project- and problem-based learning. This shift to student-centered learning requires them to act as guides and facilitators. . . . As these technology-enabled approaches gather steam, many institutions across the world are rethinking the primary responsibilities of educators. (p. 34)

At the microlevel, online educators are exploring how a change in teaching modality affects individual course designs and day-to-day teaching, but at the macrolevel, the very role of the educator itself is evolving.

If this seems daunting, consider that educators in the past have been through monumental changes such as the ones we are facing now. Over time, as information has become more and more dispersed, the primary functions, responsibilities, and duties of educators have changed. Literally, almost everyone carries around a library of information so vast it cannot even be fathomed, let alone read. The UN News Centre (2013) has reported that more people in the world have mobile phones than *toilets.* This kind of access is a momentous change in the location and availability of information. With those shifts, educators' relationships with students is also necessarily changing. It makes sense, then, that the role of educators and their primary functions, responsibilities, and duties are changing too.

Looking back over the ages, monumental transitions such as shifting from an oral to a written culture, or from a handwritten culture to a machine-written culture, seem like they happened fairly quickly and decisively, but that is only the perspective the passage of time provides. In the moment, those changes were likely gradual and bumpy, and they probably included many false starts, dead-ends, and U-turns. Educators at the individual level in previous transitional times likely felt confused, resistant, and fearful about the changes they experienced, the same way some of us feel now. They also probably felt hopeful, innovative, and excited—the same way many of us feel now.

In the face of such monumental change and the feelings of instability that change can bring, the idea of thriving professionally might sometimes feel out of reach. Thriving in a time of change is quite possible, however. One thing to keep in mind is that the roles of all educators, not just those who teach online, are changing. Another thing to keep in mind is that as an online educator, you may find that you are *better* positioned to thrive than a colleague who is still teaching only in the classroom and has not yet embraced new educational technology or teaching methods.

INVITATION TO REFLECT: EDUCATOR ROLES

Past roles of educators:

1. Imagine the role of educators in the ancient days of the oral tradition. Where was information held? As a result, what were these ancient educators' relationships with students? What were the primary functions, responsibilities, and duties of these ancient educators?

2. Imagine the role of educators before there was paper and ink, before there were printing presses. Where was information held? As a result, what were these long-ago educators' relationships with students? What were the primary functions, responsibilities, and duties of these long-ago educators?

3. Now imagine the role of college educators after printing presses, when all reading and writing was done on paper, when even students with well-endowed libraries had a limited number of educational resources at their disposal. Where was information held? As a result, what were these educators' relationships with students? What were the educators' primary functions, responsibilities, and duties?

Your changing role:

4. Which parts of these past roles appeal to you? Which excite and energize you? Which parts of these past roles do you most relate to?

5. Which parts of these past roles do not appeal to you? Do any of these past functions, responsibilities, duties, or relationships feel distasteful, intimidating, or undesirable in some way? How so? Which parts seem like they were acceptable back then but simply no longer fit the work you currently do?

6. Right now, as an online educator, how are your students different from students in the distant and not-so-distant past? In relation to your students today, how do you see your primary functions, responsibilities, and duties?

Imagining future roles:

7. Imagine a futuristic state. Conjure the setting of your favorite sci-fi novel or movie. Let your mind run wild. Make room even for fantastical ideas such as space and time travel, universal languages, robots, and artificial intelligence. How are students different in your imagined futuristic state?

8. In this futuristic setting, how do you envision the primary functions, responsibilities, and duties of educators?

THRIVING TO EFFECT CHANGE

Online educators, by embracing new technologies and experimenting with new ways of teaching, are at the forefront. As a result, our experiences and our reflections about online teaching and learning *matter* in the field of higher education right now. Openly exploring our efforts in online education is good for us professionally as individuals; reflecting, studying, and sharing our efforts in the changing field we work in is good for higher education itself.

Indeed, online educators may be uniquely positioned to have an impact on and to positively influence the course of changes happening in higher education even more broadly than merely online. The Internet has changed and continues to change how people communicate throughout many areas of our lives including personal, professional, and educational spheres. To imagine that the profound changes caused by the Internet and the information age would remain in the boundaries of the online classroom and not spread to other areas of academic life would be naïve. Our roles as educators, regardless of the modalities in which we teach, are changing because our *students* are changing in response to the vast technological breakthroughs in recent generations. Our roles are changing because *we ourselves* are changing. Online educators are at the forefront of these changes, and therefore they have a unique opportunity to thrive.

Interestingly for the online education context, Spreitzer and colleagues (2005) discussed thriving as a means of intentionally adapting ourselves to changing work environments rather than relying on external prompts and factors to exert some pressure on us that evokes a change; "[p]ut another way, thriving theorizes that individuals hold the keys to their own adaptive capacities by reading their psychological states and crafting their work in order to increase feelings of learning and energy" (p. 545). If we pay attention to the degree to which we feel vital and are learning, we can simply elect to exercise the specific behaviors noted previously to regenerate those thriving feelings if they begin to wane.

Fortunately, in many institutions the approach to delivering online education is quite collaborative. Workshops, faculty learning communities, and groups of faculty joining together for lunch-and-learn sessions about online education are happening all around us. Instructional designers, academic technologists, and media development specialists are employed by many institutions to help faculty develop and deliver high-quality online courses. These professionals are passionate about online education and academic technology and are eager to work with online educators. Often, they are the conveners of the workshops, learning communities, and other gatherings of online educators. As educators learn from these professionals and each other, the feelings of vitality can be almost palpable.

Belonging and vitality, of course, also happen in our classes among online educators and our students. Real connections happen in online classes, and although the communication is digital, it is also human. Those who argue that online classes do not have the live interactions of face-to-face classes seem to forget that those who communicate digitally are also very much alive. Although there may be excitement in the performance of a lecture and in talking with students face to face, there is also excitement when online educators pose a question and return later to find a plethora of student reactions.

Teaching an online class is in some ways simultaneously observing and participating in the creation of a text with multiple contributors. There is great joy to be found

Online educators may be uniquely positioned to positively influence changes happening in higher education, even more broadly than merely online.

#ThriveOnline

in being able to see the social construction of knowledge, to be able to view student progress through a week and through a semester. There is also great joy in helping students connect with each other, with experts, and with worlds of knowledge previously unknown to them. Many online educators also find vitality and joy in creating and sharing meaningful multimedia, which, in many corners of the Internet, are small works of art—some might even say a digital kind of folk art.

Furthermore, flourishing professionals attract others who want to experience thriving for themselves. When our work makes us feel alive and as though we are advancing in some way, we naturally want to share these feelings and the experiences that create them. Communities form. We learn from and with each other, and feelings of vitality in our work continue to grow. Whether through task focus, exploration, heedful relating, or some combination thereof, satisfaction and joy in our own careers increase.

Thriving in a time of change is not merely possible; thriving can be an important catalyst for change itself.

KEY TAKEAWAYS FROM PART TWO

- Thriving involves two aspects, emotional feelings of vitality and cognitive advances through learning.
- Rather than waiting for a sense of thriving to happen, you can intentionally evoke a sense of thriving through three kinds of behaviors: task focus, exploration, and heedful relating.

Thriving in a time of change is not merely possible; thriving can be an important catalyst for change itself.

#ThriveOnline

- Self-care, prioritizing online education activities appropriately, and establishing routines and workflows that are effective in the online asynchronous learning environment are ways to practice task focus to increase your sense of thriving.
- Formal professional development, exploring and engaging with content and social media on the Internet, and learning more about pedagogy are ways to practice exploration to cultivate a sense of thriving.
- Seeking communities with which you share a common purpose—people with whom you can heedfully relate—will help you feel connected to others and that you are part of something larger than yourself. You share common purposes with students at the class level, with colleagues at the institutional level, and with a larger community of online educators through the #ThriveOnline network.
- The Internet's information age is triggering changes in the roles of educators, online and off. Online educators, because they teach on the Internet, have unique opportunities to thrive professionally as leaders of change in higher education.

TAKE ACTION TO THRIVE

New and experienced online educators and administrators can take action to improve task focus, and to engage in exploration and heedful relations. If you are keeping a journal as you work through this book, consider writing and reflecting about the questions that follow, and consider the actions you can take to achieve a thriving state in your career.

For Educators New to Online Teaching

- Identify three strategies you employ or could employ to practice self-care to improve task focus.
- Examine a course schedule for an upcoming online course you will be teaching. Identify periods of heavier student workloads and heavier instructor workloads. Are there activities students can do more independently during your heavy grading periods? During heavy student work periods when students are concentrating on independent work and need less engagement from you, how can you make the best use of that time?
- Examine your course content. Which units or topics might benefit from additional multimedia components? Spend time exploring to find the best resources for your class, making sure you weave them into existing activities and discussions.

For Online Educators Seeking to Grow

- Analyze your teaching tasks: Which evoke feelings of vitality for you and which are most impactful for students? In contrast, which tasks do you dread? What can you adjust to make more time for the former and minimize the latter to improve your task focus?

- Reflect on your theoretical perspectives about teaching and learning. How do you believe learning happens? How does this compare with dominant views in your discipline? How do you see your role as an educator? Evaluate how well your online teaching carries out your theoretical and pedagogical perspectives.
- To feel a sense of thriving, we must continually learn. Identify some aspect of online teaching you would like to learn more about. Then, set aside time to investigate and learn.

For Administrators

- How is teaching and learning changing at your institution? How can you engage online educators to help effect positive change?
- In your role, how might you better communicate the larger purposes and goals to which a community of online educators and others can heedfully relate?
- What actions can you take to influence your institutional culture to be one where online educators feel supported in efforts to thrive?

PART THREE

HITTING YOUR STRIDE

HITTING YOUR STRIDE

When we say that people are *hitting their stride*, we mean it as a compliment, as praise for someone who is performing consistently well. The phrase is borrowed from the sport of running, and a fuller definition in that context has interesting implications for considering the profession of online teaching. Hitting your stride while running is not sprinting, going as fast as you can for a short distance. It is not a long, slow, meandering jog. Hitting your stride is an optimized tension between speed and distance, where the performance level is not only high but also enduring. To achieve this ideal state, the runner has worked to find a gait length and pace that feels natural and automatic. Runners who have hit their stride are no longer struggling with or thinking consciously about every step.

If you have ever started a running program, you know that hitting your stride is not something that happens overnight. You also know you can be a runner for quite a while before you reach the stage where you actually do hit your stride, and you are likely very familiar with what it feels like to *not* be hitting your stride, to struggle with fatigue, muscle aches, and shin splints. Perhaps you have had occasional days when the running was easy but more days when it was painful and hard and when every hill seemed only to go up. Perhaps you have been unsure if you would ever get to the point where you hit your stride.

Sometimes online educators get stuck at this point. If that happens, it can be difficult to know how to get unstuck. Interestingly, online teaching provides a unique opportunity to analyze and evaluate one's teaching, as once a class is over, the entire teaching experience is preserved and can be observed in detail by ourselves and others. In essence, every aspect of the online course design and every online interaction within a course becomes a text—a complex, multimedia text with many authors and different kinds of exchanges, but a text nonetheless. This record provides online educators with rich opportunities for reflection about our course design and teaching practices.

WHAT *NOT* HITTING OUR STRIDE LOOKS LIKE

Like archaeologists poring through a dig site, faculty developers, instructional designers, and academic technologists

Hitting your stride is an optimized tension between speed and distance.

#ThriveOnline

in charge of training and supporting online educators the world over can identify signs of professional struggle in online courses. As it turns out, when online educators are not hitting their stride, there are common tell-tale signs:

Instructor-Centered Organization of Class Materials

The course might have several folders: one for lecture materials, one for readings, one for assignments, one for exams. This makes it easy for the instructor to find materials when an update needs to be made, but students must hunt for course materials throughout the course every week. They are never exactly certain they have done everything they were supposed to do.

Too Much Text

Everything is communicated in written format, and the written format looks like a college composition paper, double-spaced Times New Roman font, not like anything you might see outside an online class on the open Web. There's no visual rhetoric and little or no multimedia. This style of presentation is comfortable and familiar for the instructor, but it is intimidating and difficult for students to parse on screen.

Too Much Lecture Content

The course might have two to four hours of lecture content each week because the instructor believes that to teach well online, the online course must mirror exactly what happens in the face-to-face version of the course. The instructor labors over writing and recording the lectures; however, the educator's lectures are in broadcast-only mode. Students are not drawn into a conversation as they might be in a campus-based classroom. They have no opportunity to ask or respond to questions. They do not even have the opportunity to use body language to look confused or bored to encourage the educator to slow down or speed up. They might be able to e-mail a question to the instructor, but they are so disengaged they are not even sure if the question is worth asking.

If educators in these kinds of courses checked the viewing statistics, they would see that many of their students stop watching before the seven-minute mark.

Lecture Content Captured From a Face-to-Face Classroom

The educator believes that lectures given in person are more engaging, so their online courses are full of lecture content recorded in a live classroom where students who are not wearing microphones ask questions that online students cannot hear clearly, and where the educator refers to assignments, exams, and due dates that may or may not apply to the online student. For the instructor, this method of delivering information is comfortable and familiar. Online students, however, feel they do not have the same access to the instructor as on-campus students, and they may be confused or frustrated by inconsistencies or inaudible content. Furthermore, if the on-campus students in the recording are identifiable and have not signed waivers, Federal Education Right to Privacy Act regulations may have been violated.

Nonfacilitated Class Discussions

There may be some text in the syllabus or elsewhere in the introductory materials of the course describing the importance of the discussions, but in classes where instructors are not hitting their strides, they are not present during the discussions, do not respond to what students are writing, and may or may not grade them in a timely fashion or at all. Instructors avoid having to learn how to facilitate a new kind of discussion but feel disconnected from students. Students participate in the discussions, but they feel they are wasting time on busy work because they perceive that the instructor is not listening or attending to them.

Hidden, Incomplete, or Confusing Gradebooks

For instructors, the online gradebook portion of the learning management system is often the most confusing and difficult to navigate. Avoiding use of this tool makes teaching simpler. However, not using the online gradebook means that the evaluation plan is a mystery to students. Grades are missing for long periods of time and then show up suddenly, often with little to no feedback. Grade columns may be titled in a confusing fashion, and students are unsure of what is being evaluated and how.

Late-Term, High-Stakes Grading

Another sign of instructors not hitting their strides in online teaching is late-term, high-stakes grading, such as evaluation plans that include only a midterm and final or one term project. For instructors, using this evaluation plan means providing less feedback to ensure an easier workload. For students, the evaluation plan is clear, but whether they are succeeding is not clear until it is too late. Midterm grades come late in the term after class withdrawal dates, or the class grades are all assigned at the end of the semester. Grading is summative only, not formative.

Not Hitting Your Stride Is Hard Work

Struggling professionally while teaching an online course using the ill-advised designs and instructional approaches discussed previously feels stiff, unnatural, impersonal, and disconnected. Educators who design and teach courses like this are not slacking, however. They are often working hard but in ineffective ways. Drafting all those written materials, writing and recording those long lectures, and grading student assignments, especially when you feel so detached from the students themselves, is tedious, arduous work. It is also not easy to respond to student complaints when they are unhappy with their grades or to their questions when it is clear they have not read or watched the material you have taken such pains to provide. This can lead to becoming irritated with students because of the ill-conceived, poorly designed learning environment. It is even understandable how some educators draw the conclusion that online teaching is just not the same and resign themselves to less than satisfactory teaching experiences. Design matters: Poor design impedes learning, but good course design promotes positive experiences for students and for the instructor.

FUNDAMENTALS FOR HITTING YOUR STRIDE: THREE FORMS OF INTERACTION

Before runners are able to hit their strides, they need some basic fundamentals to be in place, such as supportive footwear, clothing that allows free movement, warm-up and stretching activities, and practice. Likewise, there are some basic fundamentals online educators need to hit their strides.

If you are someone who is trying to try to hit your stride in online teaching, but you are not yet having success, what can you do to change the experience for your students and for yourself? Considering your course design and teaching from the student point of view, specifically students' levels of interaction throughout the course, can be a game-changer for your teaching. Since the days of telecourses, distance educators have been advised about the importance of learner interaction in online courses, specifically in three forms: student-content interaction, student-student interaction, and student-instructor interaction (Moore, 1989). Today, this advice is ubiquitous in instructor and course development materials and is often where training for online course development and

Design matters.
Good design brings
beneficial effects.
Poor design impedes
learning.

#ThriveOnline

teaching begin. Updated for the online asynchronous learning environment, the three forms of interaction model includes student-content interaction, where the students are engaged in active learning; student-student interaction, where students communicate and collaborate with each other with interest and motivation as part of a learning community; and student-instructor interaction, where students receive expert guidance and formative feedback from the instructor.

Interestingly, there is much overlap among the three forms of interaction models and arguments to increase active learning. Active learning is a method of teaching that has been in use for several decades and is perhaps most easily understood in contrast to more passive kinds of learning, where students listen to a lecture, watch a video, or read a text. In these forms of learning, students passively receive information and must recall it later. Prince (2004) argues for the effectiveness of active learning pedagogy in improving outcomes and student satisfaction in engineering education, presenting examples of active learning teaching methods, including the addition of student activity to lecture, collaborative learning, and problem-based learning. Michael (2006) categorizes the adoption of active learning pedagogy as a shift away from instructor-centered teaching toward student-centered teaching and argues that evidence demonstrates student-centered active learning pedagogy is more effective than teacher-centered methods of instruction in various scientific disciplines at the K–12 and college levels.

Active learning can be implemented in many ways but is typically defined as possessing two necessary components:

meaningful action by the students on behalf of their learning and students reflecting about their learning experience. Examples of active learning activities are plentiful and varied and include discussion activities, writing assignments, presentations, collaborative projects, and problem- and project-based learning, among others. Research has demonstrated active learning's greater effectiveness than more passive, instructor-centered styles of learning.

Student-Content Interaction and Active Learning

In passive learning situations, the instructor, video, or text presenting the content is the focal point, but in active learning, each student is central to the learning experience. Active learning theory suggests students learn better when they must perform meaningful action with the subject matter being studied. That is, students need to do more than passively receive information. They must interact with it in a meaningful way using their own sense of agency, curiosity, or purpose to learn about the content. For example, students may need to write about the content, deliver a presentation on it, address a problem related to it, or perform exercises in relation to the content such as solving math equations or completing lab activities.

In addition, students must pair that meaningful action with conscious and deliberate reflection on what and how they have learned. Reflection must happen to help students understand their own learning and to more closely acquaint them with the purpose of the learning activity.

Both components, meaningful action and reflection, are essential for active learning to occur. Interestingly, online educators can use the unique properties of the online classroom to enhance students' learning experiences with their meaningful actions and with reflection.

Meaningful Action

For action to be meaningful, the student must be motivated to engage in some way, and, here, the connection with the three forms of interaction becomes apparent: with the content, such as in computer-based learning or with a hands-on lab activity; with other students, as in peer-review writing activities; or with the instructor, as in a moderated class discussion or debate. Many variations and possibilities of activity exist. Regardless of the activity selected, in active learning each student must participate in the activity with a sense of agency and set of motivations. In face-to-face active learning activities, ensuring that each student participates meaningfully is a challenge for even the most attentive and experienced educators. The limited class meeting time and lack of technological assistance in live classrooms pose challenges and make it easier for students to fake or limit their participation. In online classes, each student logs in with a unique identifier, and the learning management system tracks and records what the student does. Each student's contributions are recorded and preserved, allowing the educator to validate quantity and quality. It is therefore much easier in the online environment for the educator to ensure each student has participated in the planned activity.

Active learning requires two components: meaningful action and reflection.

#ThriveOnline

Reflection

In addition to meaningful activity, educators must also design the learning activity to include prompts for reflection or metacognition, and these prompts ideally should do more than tell students to reflect without further guidance about what reflection is and which type of reflection to use. This means educators in all fields must learn at least a little from the discipline of education. In the student-centered online learning environment, we are no longer simply responsible for communicating information about our disciplines. To teach in student-centered ways, we need to know more about educational practices and the science of teaching and learning. In the context of reflection in active learning activities, this means learning more about what it means when we ask students to reflect. Grossman (2009) and Ryan (2012) have found that the ability to reflect as a student in higher education is not intuitive or automatic and must be explicitly taught. Grossman (2009) describes reflection as happening on a continuum, ranging from content-based reflection to transformative and intensive reflection (see Table 3.1). Ryan (2012) describes distinct levels of reflection, from reporting and responding (similar to Grossman's content-based reflection) to reconstructing (see Table 3.2).

Whether considering reflection as a continuum or as being conducted at various levels, the significance in adopting active learning strategies in our teaching is that there is more to getting students to reflect than simply telling them to reflect. Reflection is more than one thing, and depending on the teaching objectives and desired learning outcomes, students should engage in different

TABLE 3.1
Grossman's Continuum of Reflection

Reflection Type	Description
Content-based reflection	Students provide evidence and make inferences
Metacognitive reflection	Students think about their thinking, such as by distinguishing between feelings and thoughts
Self-authorship reflection	Students gain distance from earlier thinking and understand how feelings and thoughts influence each other
Transformative and intensive reflection	Students change their thoughts and feelings over time and are aware of the change

Note. Adapted from Grossman (2009).

TABLE 3.2
Ryan's Levels of Reflection

Reflection Type	Description
Reporting and responding	Students observe, describe evidence, and then ask questions or state opinions
Relating	Students make connections between content and prior learning or personal experience
Reasoning	Students analyze content, including discussions of relevant literature
Reconstructing	Students imagine future applications that may vary from current experience

Note. Adapted from Ryan (2012).

forms of reflection as appropriate for the context. Direct instruction about different kinds of reflection, as well as about how reflection assists in the learning process, is one way to guide students through successful reflective activities. Another way is to provide guiding questions that provoke the appropriate level of kind of reflection desired.

As with the meaningful action portion of active learning scenarios, the online environment may be better suited for student reflection than traditional classroom environments. Online, a host of examples of specific kinds of reflection can be provided for students to study and emulate. Students who need more time to process their reflections are not limited by rigid class meeting schedules and are not distracted by classmates sitting nearby. Additionally, students in online courses are able to share reflections using a variety of media such as text, audio, video, or sometimes even images. If a student processes information better in writing, that option is certainly available. If, however, a student is more adept at processing through speech, recording and uploading an audio or a video reflection is possible. In addition, online, students are able to share their reflections more easily and with more classmates. Finally, the online learning environment provides a clear record of student reflections over time, thus allowing students to observe transformative and intensive reflection (Grossman, 2009) in themselves and others throughout a semester or through the course of a degree program.

Challenges of Implementing Active Learning Online

Although active learning has been in the literature and in practice for decades, and educators in traditional face-to-face environments are increasingly adopting this teaching strategy, many still find it somewhat challenging to implement, even in traditional campus-based courses where all students are present in the same space at the same time. The challenge is in part because of outdated classroom designs. For example, in traditional undergraduate lecture halls, students sit in rows of immovable chairs facing forward and listen to the faculty member deliver a lecture. Requiring activity in such a restrictive physical environment can be challenging. Even in smaller classrooms with movable furniture, most students avoid the front rows and shrink toward the rear where they hope to listen passively.

Instructors of traditional face-to-face courses who desire to implement active learning strategies often must endure some social awkwardness in moving students out of the passive role and into a more active one. Most of us have been in classes or training sessions where we sit down expecting someone to lecture only to be asked to form small groups for some activity or discussion. Sometimes there is a sense of unwelcome surprise at being asked to participate. Some of that is attributable to students not knowing each other well enough to comfortably and quickly form a group, but some of that response can also be attributed to simple resistance to the call to participate. Sometimes, retraining and resetting student expectations is necessary before active learning strategies can be put in motion.

Some believe that active learning is even more difficult to implement in the asynchronous online class. Indeed, one challenge in this environment is that active learning often involves student-student interaction, with activities such as think, pair, share. Active learning strategies like these can be difficult to implement when a student may be the only person present in the online course at the time. Most of the common active learning strategies implemented in online asynchronous courses today require student-student interaction, such as whole-class discussions, small-group discussions, peer-review activities, and other collaborative assignments and projects.

Interestingly, however, the online learning environment ultimately may be *better* suited to active learning than traditional classroom-based learning. If the learning is asynchronous online, students need to take action to initiate and perpetuate the learning experience. If they sit back passively, nothing happens. To have any learning experience at all, they must navigate to the course, open the appropriate learning module, choose which aspect of the class to interact with, click to open and read files, participate in tutorials and simulations, and compose messages to contribute to class discussions and to complete assessments. Unlike many campus-based students, online students come to class expecting a certain level of agency and participation.

Additionally, online students have significantly more autonomy in selecting the order of their participation, the duration of time they spend participating, and whether their participation time is in long sessions or multiple short sessions. As a result, online students more willingly overcome resistance to active learning, not because of innate differences between the online and traditional student populations, but simply because the online environment requires the student to take a more active role. The nature of the medium requires student action to function.

When confronted with the myth that online classes are easier than campus-based courses, veteran online students often remark that they find online classes to be more difficult than on-campus courses. Their reasons are that they must have better time management skills and be self-motivated, which are certainly factors that contribute to the difficulty. Perhaps, though, another factor is that in online classes that are designed well, students must play a more active role. Perhaps well-designed online classes demand more of them.

This is not to suggest that the online learning environment automatically or naturally creates an active learning environment. According to Michael (2006), "[A]ctive learning does not just happen; it occurs in the classroom when the teacher creates a learning environment that makes it more likely to occur" (p. 164). The same is true in the online classroom. In fact, this is one of the main reasons substantial training in designing and delivering online courses is necessary. Distinct design and facilitation strategies are needed to create an active learning environment online (Box 3.1).

Box 3.1 Online Active Learning Checklist

Design strategies to promote active learning in online courses:

- Make learning objectives explicit to help students understand the purpose of the activity and to prime the pump for metacognition.
- Test directions for potential users and update them as needed when educational technology changes. Screenshots can often be helpful.
- Recognize that interaction is not instantaneous in online asynchronous classes and build in response times that take adult learner work schedules into account; often this means including at least one weekend in the activity time frame.
- Provide direct instruction for the kind of reflection you want students to undertake.
- Designate a question-and-answer area and encourage students to respond to each other's questions if they can to help reduce students' wait times for assistance.
- Develop detailed rubrics that include guidance for the activity and reflection portions of the active learning experience.

Facilitation strategies to promote active learning in online courses:

- Provide advance notice for active learning activities, especially if they require extra time or otherwise disrupt the established routine of class participation.
- Call class attention to positive exemplars midactivity to provide additional guidance for those who need it.
- Notice where students get confused with directions and amend them for future iterations of the class.

(Continues)

Box 3.1 (*Continued*)

- Remind students of the learning objectives, such as by calling attention to aspects of the activity or reflection that might apply in future educational or professional contexts.
- Provide prompt, constructive feedback as needed during the activity.
- Provide synthesizing and evaluative feedback as soon as possible after the activity is complete.

STUDENT-STUDENT INTERACTION: HIGH-IMPACT COLLABORATIVE LEARNING

Several forms of student-content interaction have been discussed, as well as several examples of student-student interaction, which of course also relates to course content. An important variety of active learning that uses student-student interaction is collaborative learning, which is recommended by the Association of American Colleges & Universities' (AAC&U's) Liberal Education and America's Promise (LEAP) initiative, which seeks to bring a liberal education to more college students regardless of discipline. It includes principles of excellence as well as several categories of learning objectives: knowledge of culture and the physical world, intellectual and practical skills, personal and social responsibility, and integrative and applied learning (Kuh, 2008). A central part of the LEAP initiative is a collection of high-impact practices, that is, teaching and learning practices that have been shown to be effective for student learning, especially for students from underrepresented, first-generation, and disadvantaged backgrounds.

The high-impact practice of collaborative learning "combines two key goals: learning to work and solve problems in the company of others, and sharpening one's own understanding by listening seriously to the insights of others, especially those with different backgrounds and life experiences" (Kuh, 2008, para. 7). Collaborative learning is sometimes conflated with cooperative learning, but they are distinct. Stahl, Koschmann, and Suthers (2014) state that in cooperative learning, "learning is done by individuals, who then contribute their individual results and present the collection of individual results as their group product," whereas collaboration requires students to engage in "group interactions like negotiation and sharing . . . with a shared task that is constructed and maintained by and for the group" (p. 481). Cooperative and collaborative learning can help online educators implement active learning activities for their online classes, but more rigorous collaborative learning helps students also meet the LEAP learning objectives related to intellectual and practical skills, such as critical and creative thinking, as well as teamwork and problem-solving (Kuh, 2008).

Examples of collaborative assignments for online asynchronous courses might include many familiar ones from the on-campus environment, as well as others especially well suited for the online environment such as group papers, presentations, and projects; case studies; websites; annotated electronic portfolios; infographics; digital time lines; paired programming or problem-solving; and

Online students come to class expecting a certain level of agency and participation.

#ThriveOnline

INVITATION TO REFLECT: IMPLEMENTING ACTIVE LEARNING ONLINE

1. Consider a place in your course where students currently receive information passively, such as through watching a video or completing an assigned course reading. List three meaningful actions students could take in relation to this content in the online environment.

2. Next, list three ways you could modify the current design of your course to require students to reflect on what or how they learned in completing one or more of these actions in the online environment. Remember to provide direct instructions about the kind of reflection you want students to practice. Be specific.

Invitation to Connect

Choose an activity you could use in your class. Choose a reflection assignment that would work well with your activity. Share your results with your #ThriveOnline community.

photojournalism or digital storytelling projects, among others. To be truly collaborative instead of merely cooperative, the creation of the group's project should require planning, negotiation, discussion, or other tasks or communications that cannot effectively be accomplished by an individual member in isolation.

Like other active learning approaches, collaborative learning may be challenging to implement initially in an online asynchronous environment but ultimately may be better suited for online environments than through the face-to-face modality. The asynchronous online learning environment can be used to maximize the effectiveness of collaborative learning activities through documenting group planning, negotiations, discussions, and other communications. Progress between project milestones or from draft to draft can be recorded, observed, and reflected on more thoroughly and conveniently. Perhaps most significant from the classroom management perspective, individual contributions and participation can be more easily documented, observed, and accounted for in grading.

Implementing collaborative learning can be challenging in online asynchronous courses. Robertson and Riggs (2017) outline several challenges for implementation within online asynchronous courses, including schedule incompatibilities, communication issues, technical difficulties, and assessment challenges. However, instructors can use design and facilitation strategies to implement this useful high-impact practice to create a student-centered learning environment in online asynchronous courses.

Design and Facilitation Strategies for Online Collaborative Learning

The following strategies can help you design effective collaborative learning activities for asynchronous online classes and will help relieve stresses commonly associated with collaborative learning, allowing students to focus on meeting learning objectives.

- Allow sufficient time for adult learners to collaborate, including planning, drafting, deliberation, and revision.
- Suggest or require interim milestones with clear deliverables prior to the final project due date to help motivate and coordinate groups.
- Create low- or no-stakes assessments that use the same educational technology used in big projects to help troubleshoot technical difficulties before the big project is due.
- Clarify in advance how grades will be handled in cases of low or no participation, when a group member disappears from the course, or when a group member is late with part of the group work and provide clear reporting structures for such eventualities.
- Design reflective aspects of the assignment such as process or learning journals, metacognitive cover letters or memos, or video project introductions that present lessons learned, examples of transformed thinking, or descriptions of the collaborative process.

Collaborative learning is an attractive high-impact practice for online educators who wish to create student-centered learning environments because it can be used in any discipline and in almost any class size and because it encourages students to develop the critical thinking and communication skills that are important in many professions. However, collaborative learning does have its challenges. When teaching an online course that requires collaborative learning, the following facilitation strategies can help prevent and address common concerns:

- Provide direct instruction on collaboration expectations. Require communication that is visible to the educator (e.g., in a small-group discussion forum or shared storage drive) to help students document collaboration for accountability and reflection purposes.
- Provide direct instruction on conflict resolution to help students understand the value of conflict and negotiate disagreements constructively.
- Make the relevance of the collaborative work to students' educational and professional goals explicit so that students understand the learning advantages of collaboration.
- Maintain a visible presence in group communications and provide prompt feedback to mini milestone deliverables and questions from group members.

Collaborative learning can be implemented in significant ways, such as with long-term group projects, as already discussed, as well as in shorter term applications, such as in whole-class or small-group online asynchronous discussions, or in peer-review activities where students focus on individual papers or projects and instructors weave collaboration into otherwise individual work as a required step in the process. Benefits of collaborative learning include social, psychological, and cognitive advantages such as providing a vehicle for the development of critical thinking skills; increased motivation to participate in rigorous active learning experiences; additional opportunities to engage with diverse others; and feelings of belonging to and having a responsibility for a learning community, which can encourage learners to persist.

STUDENT-INSTRUCTOR INTERACTION

One of the biggest misconceptions of faculty new to online education, and perhaps the most potentially damaging for the student learning experience, is the belief that student-instructor interaction happens less frequently, with less authenticity, or with less intensity in the online environment. Instructors who are skeptical and critical of online education most often hold these negative views because they believe they would have less interaction with students in the online environment and because they—rightfully—understand their interaction with students as critical to the learning experience. The misguided assumption that student-instructor interaction is lesser in online asynchronous environments can lead some fledgling online educators and their unfortunate students to experience an overall failure to thrive in the online environment.

Student-instructor interaction in online asynchronous courses begins long before students are present in the class. It begins when the online educator is set to design and develop the online course and must imagine how students will interact with the content and each other, as well as with the educators themselves in the future.

Even before the students are present in the online course, they are present in the educator's mind. Pedagogical approaches are selected and implemented, course materials are sequenced to build more complex concepts on more foundational information, and the educator anticipates what students will need to be successful while attempting to strike the right tension between educator support and students' struggles to optimize the learning experience.

Once students are enrolled and present in the online class, interaction with the instructor continues to be important, as discussed previously in relation to educator participation in online asynchronous discussions, for example, and in the effective creation of media content for some courses. Educators who have successfully made the transition from teaching in a brick-and-mortar space to an online environment often share a common but surprising realization about online teaching; that is, they interact more regularly and with greater numbers of individual students online than was possible in their on-campus classes.

Providing Feedback

Another moment when critical student-instructor interaction happens is when the online educator responds to student work. Providing feedback on student work as an instructional practice is important in all learning modalities. Receiving rich, detailed, and timely feedback is highly valued by most students. However, in the absence of synchronous communication, where students are better able to self-assess their development, progress, and levels of understanding by comparing their reactions to class activities and content to those of other class members in the moment, instructor feedback on student work is likely more critical for student learning in the online setting.

Although sometimes challenging to deliver, as with active and collaborative learning, providing rich, detailed, and timely feedback may ultimately be better suited to the online environment than to others. In online learning environments, educators can use technological assistance such as text replacement software (e.g., ShortKeys or aText) to provide detailed feedback including links to helpful URLs, references to specific page numbers in a course text, or detailed explanations the instructor custom creates. Although some feedback on student work is highly individualized, patterns of mistakes in student work may result in an overlap in the feedback needed by multiple students in any given class. Text replacement software allows instructors to supply feedback that would need to be repeated for more than one student simply by typing brief codes or snippets of text. The software then automatically replaces the brief snippet with preprogrammed feedback that is fuller and more detailed. Although this kind of software will not handle all typed feedback, as some will need to be individualized, it does significantly improve grading efficiency and allows educators to provide more detailed feedback more consistently.

Other technologies that can be easily adopted in the online learning environment by educators who are eager to embrace the medium include automated feedback on computer-graded questions such as multiple choice. In designing a quiz, for example, most learning management systems will allow autograding of tests, which can be returned immediately or at a specific date and time, and customizing brief explanations to help students understand why certain answers were wrong. These automatic explanations can be used to redirect students to online tutorials, specific pages in a textbook, or other study aids. More advanced educational technologies, such as branching tutorials or adaptive learning software, automatically adjust to students' levels and redirect them to earlier concepts or automatically advance them more quickly based on their responses, in the learning moment, so they do not have to wait days or weeks to receive helpful feedback.

Some educators find it effective and efficient to provide video or audio feedback on student assignments, and the online learning environment makes it easy to do so. In some learning management systems, this functionality is built in. Other free educational technologies make it easy to provide such feedback in any system simply by providing the recording's URL. For example, Screencast-O-Matic allows educators to capture video recordings of student assignments on screen while also providing the educator's edits, markups, and voice-over commentary as they happen. It would be very difficult to provide this kind of feedback in face-to-face classes, given the time constraints of face-to-face meeting schedules, but doing so online is easy and efficient with the use of the right technologies.

Furthermore, assignments collected and graded digitally can be graded and returned quickly and efficiently, often sooner than the next scheduled meeting time in a face-to-face environment. Brief extensions of due dates can also be accommodated within tighter time frames as desired and appropriate.

Invitation to Connect

What is your favorite interaction or efficiency tool for the online environment? Share your recommendations with the #ThriveOnline community.

Beyond Fundamentals: Achieving Fluency in Online Education

When people learn a second language and become competent enough in reading, writing, listening, and speaking in the new language that they can communicate with ease even with native speakers, we say they have achieved *fluency*. In running, as previously discussed, we call this heightened state of advanced and enduring performance *hitting our stride*, a state in which we are no longer consciously aware of each step. Motion feels fluid and natural. In language acquisition, this level of expertise happens when second-language speakers no longer need to translate their native language into the new language and vice versa. They access the new language automatically and are so immersed they often even think in the new language. Furthermore, fluent speakers of second languages often have absorbed some of the other culture as well as the language itself. Idiomatic expressions unique to that language are untranslatable yet feel organic and make perfect sense.

How can online educators move beyond the fundamentals of student-content, student-student and student-

INVITATION TO REFLECT: STUDENT-INSTRUCTOR INTERACTION

1. Have you experienced the surprising realization that well-designed and facilitated online courses lead to more student-instructor interaction than many face-to-face courses? What specifically prompted this surprising realization for you?

2. If you have not yet experienced this realization in your own teaching, where in your course do you see potential to increase or improve student-instructor interaction?

instructor interaction? How can they master the online space naturally and with ease the way fluent speakers of other languages do?

Beyond the three forms of interaction, one of the first things online educators who are thriving have figured out is that trying to create a mirror image of their on-campus course is a mistake and that the materials they use in person in their face-to-face classes do not stand on their own inside the online course very well. They discover that clinging too tightly to what they know about face-to-face teaching can sometimes be a barrier to teaching well online. Over time, they find that the online course needs to be designed and facilitated in a way that makes the best possible use of the online medium. When online educators embrace the online medium rather than struggle against it, they achieve fluency and hit their stride.

Embracing the online medium means that educators are familiar enough with the customs and functionality of the Internet to marshal its power for the good of teaching and learning. Very much like fluent speakers of a second language, or runners who have hit their stride, they perform at consistently high levels, seeming to intuit which are the right tools and rhythms needed to maximize student learning. Online educators who hit their strides share three things in common:

1. They understand the properties of the Internet and how they apply to online education.
2. They know what they can do better online than they can face to face.
3. They know the shortcomings of the medium, and they work to counteract them.

Understanding Properties of the Internet and Implications for Online Teaching

Because the Internet is so vast, attempting to define it may seem like hubris. The Internet contains all kinds of content in every language and file format imaginable. Even so, it is possible to identify several of its specific properties. Educators who hit their strides in online teaching understand the essential properties of the Internet and their implications for online teaching.

The Internet Is Vast, Yet Portable

The Internet provides access to massive amounts of information, more than any one person could absorb in a lifetime, and it grows exponentially every day. Paradox-ically, while the Internet is growing, it is also becoming increasingly portable, which means people can learn, participate, connect, and contribute content everywhere they go. Information on the Internet is presented in multimedia format, including text, images, sound, video, and even in immersive 3D virtual reality. The Internet is user centered and invites participation and connection. The medium is not broadcast only the way television is. Users are invited to write as well as contribute content in other ways, such as by creating and sharing images, audio recordings, and videos. Finally, many find signifi-cant satisfaction in sharing ideas, experiences, and mul-timedia creations with others who react and respond to this content in myriad ways.

The expansive nature of the Internet and the improv-ing portability of devices used to access it mean that learning is no longer contained within the walls of a classroom or library. Students can and do learn anytime, anywhere. Learning is part of daily life, at least poten-tially, and is not relegated to a particular course, degree program, or even a particular phase of life. We are all consumers of information and lifelong learners. For edu-cators, access has several implications. Our students will participate in our online classes at all times of the day and night and as their schedules allow, so we must let go of course calendars that are tied to traditional class-room schedules and create schedules that make sense for online asynchronous nontraditional learners. For example, rather than posting a day-by-day list of tasks, post the list by week, unit, or module. Allow students to determine how best to manage their time within that framework.

Indeed, using the Internet in their daily lives means that students will expect to have more choice and autonomy. For example, our students no longer simply listen to the radio. Fully accustomed to digitally connected living, they listen to music on the Internet where they create their own stations and playlists and modify them by indicating the tracks they like and combining artists or genres. News does not even need to be listened to live; instead, we download and listen to it as podcasts on our own schedules. To a certain degree, learning management systems can allow us to manipulate settings to force students through rigid sequences. However, building choice into our course designs will make our online courses more comfortable for our digitally native students.

The growth of Internet access also means the educator is no longer the student's main delivery source for information. Educator-provided information can be quickly and easily supplemented, enhanced, fact checked, updated, and even supplanted. We should acknowledge the wealth of information available and help our students learn to assess what they find and help connect them to the best of what we find. Sometimes this means we need to set aside our own lecture notes in favor of another source that is more expertly or meaningfully presented. Our role then becomes one of integrating content with learning activities, contextualizing information in our class, and helping students probe and engage.

Production Value Matters

In the media-rich environment of the Internet, online courses are competing with viral videos, animations, GIFs, memes, professionally produced websites, and messaging that have been carefully designed to carry the greatest possible impact with the lowest possible cognitive load. Those teaching in this environment may be overreliant on PowerPoint presentations and unprepared to develop the rich, polished, and professional media content to which students are becoming accustomed. This means faculty will find it worthwhile to spend valuable course preparation time improving media production value or at least curating and integrating content that has academic quality and high production value. Relying on text alone or on voicing over endless bulleted lists on slides will not be sufficient.

Interaction Is Expected

The environment of the Internet also means that students accustomed to inhabiting this space expect to be able to participate and connect with others at will. Many will hunger for response, reaction, and interaction, because communication with others is the norm for this medium. Therefore, our course designs should invite interaction, sharing, and response. Furthermore, in our facilitation of online courses, we must realize the importance of our own interaction in the form of discussion, synthesis, monitoring the progress of each student, personalization of the learning experience, guided inquiry, and frequent and timely feedback on student work. Online courses require much from educators in terms of careful, attentive facilitation.

The Internet Is a User-Centered Space

Perhaps most significant, if we are to embrace the online medium, we must understand the Internet as a user-centered space. *User centered* means something is designed in a way to help people achieve their goals by understanding their work flows, anticipating their needs, and creating environments that streamline their efforts. It also means the design takes into account how people *actually* tend to behave rather than how the designer *thinks* they should behave and adjusts the design accordingly. Clarity in content and navigation and offering people choices in how they interact in a space are also key components of user centeredness, as are iteration and continual refinement over time.

We know the Internet is a user-centered space because people who decide to use it determine what sites they visit, how they interact, how long they stay, and how much of their attention they devote to any site or a portion thereof. Furthermore, choices are not merely navigational; the Internet invites and encourages participation and creation and users decide how to con-tribute and interact. This is how sites such as YouTube, Facebook, Twitter, Instagram, LinkedIn, and countless blogs have become treasure troves of content as well as cultural phenomena. Users create profiles, create and share content, and share and comment on content made by others. Whole communities are formed around areas of interest, and people interact in meaningful ways. Designers constantly streamline and revise content and add functionality to make information easier to absorb and to make interaction simultaneously richer and easier to accomplish.

The Internet has become as important and natural a medium for communication as speaking, writing a letter, or making a phone call was for previous generations. Our students spend a lot of time online, and they know this environment well. To teach well in this learning environment, we must know how the growth of and increased access to the Internet have affected our students as learners and what it suggests for our roles as educators in this space.

User-Centered Means Student-Centered in Online Classrooms

The Internet's user-centered nature in particular has important implications for online education. Because the Internet is a user-centered space, as we move educational environments online, we must create them as user-centered—that is, student-centered—spaces. Online educators who design courses in instructor-centered fashion are working against the innate qualities of the online medium and therefore make their teaching objectives more difficult to accomplish. If, however, online educators fully recognize the potential of putting our classes on the Internet and embrace the Internet's innate properties—that is, if we learn to design and teach courses in student-centered ways—we are more likely to thrive.

EMBRACING THE MEDIUM FOR WHAT IT ACCOMPLISHES BETTER

Online educators have a firm understanding of the properties of the Internet as well as the implications for online teaching, and those who thrive in the online environment have discovered what needs to be and can be done better. Instead of trying to create imitations of what we do on campus, online educators who are thriving ask, "What can the online medium do better than can be done face to face? What can it do that is unique?" See Box 3.2 and Box 3.3 (later in this chapter) for some suggested strategies and experiences to enhance your online teaching practice and student experience.

Reflection, Metacognition, and Critical Thinking

As discussed earlier in the context of active learning, reflection is one thing we can often do better online than in person because the online asynchronous environment allows students to use as much time as they would like and to make as many attempts as needed to learn and reflect on course content. Students can also find benefits in examining the reflections of fellow students as they consider their own reflections. Over time, metacognition is also easier to conduct online, as students are able to track their own changing thought processes and compare their own thought processes side by side with those of others.

Similarly, if designed and facilitated well, online courses can be better for building critical thinking skills because they allow students to work at their own pace,

---

Box 3.2 Interaction Checklist

Interaction will vary from course to course and even within a single course. The checklist that follows provides reflective questions to help you identify how to improve interaction in your online courses and meet your students' expectations for interaction in the online medium:

- In your discussion participation, have you encouraged synthesis of ideas by weaving together threads from several individual student posts?
- Have you helped students draw connections between course resources and their discussion contributions and assignments?
- In your feedback to students, do you reference progress since or connections with previous assignments?
- Have you provided opportunities for students to customize assignments and projects based on their professional goals and individual interests?
- Have you modeled or provided direct instruction on critical thinking and problem-solving skills?
- Have you provided some open-ended questions or explorations?
- Have you communicated and abided by assignment feedback deadlines, such as responding to questions within 24 hours and returning graded work within 5 days?

---

review content as many times as necessary, and access supporting resources if needed. For the purposes of critical thinking, face-to-face courses can be like live performances, where certain passages can be missed and it is impossible to take in all aspects of the performance at once. Paying close attention to one actor means paying less to others, to the set, and so on. To extend this analogy, online courses are like recorded performances that can be replayed, thus allowing students to repeat what they missed and consider various perspectives in turn. In addition, online, asynchronous courses can be designed to require critical thinking of all students individually, even in whole-class discussions, whereas an evenly distributed critical thinking practice can be nearly impossible to achieve in face-to-face class discussions in which some students eagerly participate but others abstain.

Diversity

Along the same lines, online courses may also be more successful than campus-based courses at bringing diverse groups of students together, thus enhancing critical thinking practice through exposure to additional perspectives and life experiences. In online education's early days, student populations tended to be nontraditional working adults returning to school to finish a degree or adults seeking a career change who often were also balancing family responsibilities, work, and school. Over time, however, more and more traditional students in the 18 to 22 age range have been opting for online courses. According to the Survey of Online Learning (Allen et al., 2016), 28% of undergraduates now take at least 1 online course in the pursuit of their degrees. For institutions that allow students to pursue degree programs with a combination of on-campus, hybrid or blended, and online courses, this means at least a potentially more diverse student body in online courses where nontraditional students are increasingly participating in courses with traditional students. One way online educators can thrive is to recognize and find ways to make educational use of the diversity in their classes.

Online courses can also bring together students from different geographical regions, ethnic and religious groups, ages, levels of experience and varying professional backgrounds, and other diverse populations into one course. Because online courses can be helpful for interpersonal reasons, and exposure to more perspectives opens our minds to a wider variety of experiences and data, they can also be more diverse in terms of content, especially in subjects such as natural resources, geography, sustainability, local government, and culture where students share information and resources from their regions.

INVITATION TO REFLECT: DIVERSITY

Choose one of your courses. How might the diversity of your students be used to improve the learning experience more intentionally?

Invitation to Connect
Share your thoughts about diversity in your online class with the #ThriveOnline community.

Laboratories

Although some perceive labs as being especially difficult to deliver online, advances in educational technology and multimedia development are making online labs easier to achieve. With experience, online educators often find that there are distinct advantages in delivering lab courses and activities online as opposed to face to face. Kennepohl (2016) described the pedagogical challenges of science: "In the sciences, learners are expected to state problems; ask questions; make observations; keep records; offer explanations; create, design, or carry out experiments; reevaluate hypotheses; and communicate findings" (p. 2). Among these learning activities, carrying out laboratory experiments is commonly seen as the most challenging to accomplish online. Kennepohl (2016), however, sees the challenges of teaching sciences online as similar to the challenges of teaching other disciplines online, that is, as "instructional design problems and therefore susceptible to instructional design solutions" (p. ix). Kennepohl (2016) offers foundational chapters in teaching biology, chemistry, earth science, and physics online, followed by case studies exploring such topics as computer simulations, remote access lab equipment, and field- and lab-based curricula.

Of course, not every lab can be conducted online; for example, labs that call for handling hazardous materials or expensive, specialized equipment must still be taught in traditional laboratory environments. Interestingly, however, given adequate course development and the application of effective instructional design solutions, the online delivery of science courses, including labs, can

Because the Internet is a *user-centered* space, online courses should be designed as *student-centered* spaces.

#ThriveOnline

sometimes be better online than in some traditional face-to-face environments. How so? As with reflection and critical thinking, students are able to view foundational content and supplemental resources repeatedly, in whole or in part. When students use simulations, costs over time in terms of damage, wear and tear, and downtime can be reduced when expensive lab equipment is harmed. Online, a student error is easy to correct with no permanent harm done. Online student errors can also be easier to record and therefore easier to identify and apply interventions to correct. In addition, online delivery of labs allows randomization of variables, which can simulate real-world conditions better than carefully controlled traditional laboratory settings.

Furthermore, the online delivery of labs can be arranged to require each student to participate more easily than in traditional labs, which, for reasons related to time, space, and course enrollment capacity, are often conducted with pairs or small groups of students. Delivering labs online means potentially fewer free riders and a greater number of fully engaged students. Part of embracing the Internet is being willing to see such benefits and to take advantage of them, even when it may mean challenging what has been until now the exclusive reign of traditional methods.

Multimedia

Of course, online classrooms are far better equipped for sharing multimedia content than analog brick-and-mortar classrooms. Although educators can certainly show a video or visit a website in a face-to-face class, the technical challenges involved in doing so are often prohibitive. Problems with network access, speaker malfunctions, outdated classroom computers, and Wi-Fi interruptions, among other technical challenges, can add up to significant amounts of wasted class time. Even when everything works properly, ensuring the entire class can see and hear clearly, pays attention, and catches everything in one viewing is a tall order. The distribution of media is much more efficient when accessed individually in the user's own customized environment. Online students are able to pay attention to media content in their classes on their own schedules, perhaps using commuting hours to listen to recordings or viewing lecture content during a workday lunch break. Being able to select the time and space they can devote to media content can help students make the most of their limited time and attention.

In online classrooms, just as in on-campus classrooms, it can be difficult to guarantee that students are paying careful attention to multimedia content. However, instructional design measures can be adopted to mitigate this challenge and to measure the effectiveness and clarity of multimedia course materials. For example, embedding graded comprehension questions into video content can help faculty verify that students viewed and understood course materials presented in video format. Over time, faculty can gather data based on student responses to quiz questions to assess the effectiveness of the media object in conveying the necessary information. Alternative media objects can even be tested against each other. Measures can be taken to gather efficacy data on campus; however, online usage statistics and quiz responses can be built into the delivery platform and may make such data easier to collect.

In addition, using multimedia that students create is also easier to do in the online learning environment where such artifacts can usually be shared as easily as copying and pasting a link to a public area of a class. Putting students in the role of creating and sharing media content increases students' experience with active learning and adds a layer of accountability and engagement that can be missing from face-to-face courses, especially larger enrollment courses. Again, these kinds of learning activities can be added on to face-to-face courses; however, online learning management systems have media sharing built into the online classroom, so usage can be more convenient and more authentic in the online setting.

Integrating Internet-Based Information Into Student Life

When students are in an online course, they are a browser tab away from accessing massive amounts of information from a wide variety of sources and perspectives. An online class is better than a face-to-face course in incorporating those resources into class learning activities. Students can be asked to find, reference, compare, dispute, critique, evaluate, share, adapt, or respond to online sources. Using the tools built into the learning management system itself, students can easily identify, access, and share resources and information that is personally relevant to their own unique interests in the course subject matter and to their own personal and professional goals.

The growing portability of Internet access provides another important consideration, as online students can be asked to go out into their environments and take photos or video recordings to document field observations or progress through lab activities or techniques they are practicing, such as postures or physical motions for clinical coursework. In addition to finding resources, students can create them.

Beyond resources, though, courses can be designed to require that students interact with and reflect on course topics in highly personalized ways. For example, students in business or psychology courses can reflect on the application or observation of principles or theories learned in class in their own lives and workplaces soon after they happen, such as on a lunch or coffee break, sharing their real-world experiences with the rest of the class. Students in computer science courses can create databases and apps that can be used in their professional and volunteer lives. The Internet can bring resources into an online class, but online educators who have hit their stride realize that it can also be used to bring the online class into the world, whenever and wherever students go. With online learning, the class environment no longer has to be something you leave your life to attend. Instead, it can be something you bring with you into your life.

INVITATION TO REFLECT: YOUR CLASS IN THE WORLD

You have no doubt already thought about resources you can bring into your class. Reverse this thinking. Where in the world might your students be able to bring your class?

Personalized Learning

Much attention and expense are being dedicated right now to efforts to personalize education and improve student retention and success rates. Online courses can be better suited to personalizing student learning than classroom-based courses. Often when educators and administrators talk about personalized learning, they are referring to software available for licensing or purchase from vendors. Certainly, the online classroom makes it easy to incorporate personalized educational software. Software such as Pearson's MyMathLab or McGraw-Hill's ALEKS platforms supply math problems for students, require that students show their work, and provide instant feedback on student work. Additionally, this software assesses student understanding of specific skills and concepts and adjusts accordingly, such as by advancing students who have demonstrated mastery to the next concept or by redirecting students who are struggling to more introductory materials with which they need more practice.

Interestingly, Feldstein and Hill (2016) take a broader view and conversely consider the personalization of education to be a practice rather than a product:

> We can start by taking a hard look at course designs and identifying those areas that fail to make meaningful individual contact with students. These gaps will be different from course to course, subject to subject, student population to student population, and teacher to teacher. Although there is no generic answer to the question of where students are most likely to fall through the cracks in a course, there are some patterns. (para. 5)

All online courses that are developed and facilitated by educators who have embraced the Internet have at least the potential of personalizing the learning experience for every student the way Feldstein and Hill recommend—that is, as process not product. Personalizing learning is not as simple as making a purchase or adopting a technology-assisted exercise into a class; it is developing and refining a whole new student-centered approach to teaching and learning. The online asynchronous nature of courses and availability to share found and created information are the are qualities that lend themselves well to personalization, if they are designed and facilitated in that manner.

Educators who embrace the Internet recognize that online learners expect to participate, and they can design courses that invite and require learners to participate. Personalizing the learning experience builds on the foundation of participation by providing more options for student participation or, in some cases, by guiding students through a process where they design their own learning experiences, such as with project-based learning. To personalize a business course, for example, students may simply be given a choice among case studies situated in different industries or international settings. Such choices provide students with the opportunity to meet their own learning goals. As they study basic principles of economics or management, for instance, they can consider them in contexts that will help them explore vastly different industrial or cultural settings. Using project-based learning, students may be required to propose a unique project to meet a given set of learning outcomes in a highly personalized manner. For example, students may need to

Box 3.3 What Can We Do Better Online?

Individual learning experiences will vary and much depends on course design and facilitation, but following are some teaching and learning experiences that can be especially effective in the online environment:

- Reflection, metacognition, and critical thinking activities can be structured and modeled online. Students can engage in these activities on their own time, free from distraction, and can share their reflective work in a variety of formats.
- Online courses have the potential of attracting a diverse body of students from different parts of the world and cultural backgrounds and from a wide variety of ages and levels of experience. Well-designed online courses leverage this diversity to improve learning experiences.
- Labs can be designed using complex technologies such as simulations or with simple household supplies. Well-designed online labs require more individual engagement and active learning than most timed group activities in campus-based settings.
- Multimedia components can be used, created, and shared using tools built into the online classroom with great ease.
- Resources from the Internet can easily be integrated into online learning experiences.
- Evidence of student learning can be shared with other students and the instructor easily and in a variety of formats, making it easier to assess students and ensure accountability.

(Continues)

Box 3.3 (*Continued*)

> - Students can bring online courses with them into the real world such as in fieldwork, observations, and professional settings.
> - Personalized learning educational technologies and pedagogical approaches can be easier to manage and assess online.

demonstrate mastery of business-writing concepts related to writing an analytical report by creating an authentic business-related reason requiring written analysis, conducting research, and writing the analysis in a clear and persuasive style suitable for the intended audience. With this kind of assignment, students have tremendous flexibility in personalizing the rhetorical situation, the research, and so on, while meeting the same learning objectives related to business writing.

Regardless of the discipline and pedagogical approach, tracking student activity and success is crucial. Well-designed online courses taught by faculty who have been trained to analyze course data can help us identify the patterns mentioned by Feldstein and Hill (2016) and can help us use evidence-based approaches to personalize education for more students more often.

COUNTERACTING THE MEDIUM'S SHORTCOMINGS

In addition to understanding the properties of the Internet and the implications for online teaching, and awareness of what we can accomplish better teaching on the Internet than we can in face-to-face environments, online educators who are hitting their strides are also aware of the online medium's shortcomings.

Although there are many advantages to online teaching and learning, the rise of digital connectedness has certainly not been all positive. Online educators who are thriving are realistic in their appraisals of these shortcomings and intentionally strive to counteract them. For example, in many places on the Internet, a lack of civility is problematic. Visit the comments section of an online local news article about an even remotely controversial topic and it is easy to observe some truly abhorrent behaviors. In addition, some media and social media outlets seem to have what has been termed an *echo chamber* effect, resulting in users being isolated from multiple perspectives and falsely led to believe in the veracity or supremacy of one viewpoint. Unfortunately, some students allow these uncivil and countereducational practices to follow them into the online classroom. Accordingly, online educators must preempt these behaviors and harmful practices by crafting and enforcing online etiquette policies for online courses, especially if the courses touch on controversial or politically charged topics or if your institution's student conduct code is campus centric and not specific enough to address digital communication.

Another challenge of the online medium is that amateurs can craft messages that look professional. As a result, it can be more difficult to know if the information is credible. With the proliferation of media development tools and access, it is easier for dishonest and unethical

INVITATION TO REFLECT: STRENGTHS OF THE ONLINE MEDIUM

1. What other aspects of the online medium do you see as potential strengths for the purposes of higher education?
2. What might you be able to do better online than you have been able to do in face-to-face settings?

people to manipulate and deceive others. Teaching information literacy, especially as it pertains to information obtained online, is critical. We can no longer afford to isolate these skills to one or two general education courses, as deceitful communicators improve in their abilities to craft professional and credible-looking messages on a regular and ongoing basis. Educators must be attuned to the latest tactics and must teach students how to guard themselves against manipulation. Resources such as the Purdue University Online Writing Lab's (2018) webpage provide guidance for assessing the credibility of sources, such as identifying the author, the date of publication, and analysis of the author's purpose in writing.

In addition, copying and pasting, sharing, and forwarding are as easy as the click of a button. In many ways, the ease of sharing information can be beneficial; however, there needs to be sufficient time for cognitive processing, evaluation, or reflection. As educators in this digital space, we must realize that our students need direct instruction about, and practice with, critical thinking, verification skills, reflection, and metacognition. We need to build processes into our online classroom management that guide students to slow down, think, and assess before sharing.

THE JOYS OF ONLINE TEACHING

Hitting our strides as online educators of course includes course designs and pedagogical strategies that are advantageous for students, whether those be the fundamentals of student-content, student-student, and student-instructor interaction or the instructor's more advanced levels of facility with the online environment orchestrated for the benefit of students. But what about advantages from the *educator's* point of view? Is it selfish or otherwise in poor form to consider in a professional space effectiveness and satisfaction for the instructor?

Runners are not motivated to do the work involved to hit their strides only for health benefits. Rather, hitting their strides is *pleasurable*. The pleasure of running well motivates runners to continue the activity and to overcome challenges such as fatigue or injury. Likewise, the pleasure of teaching well online can motivate educators to do the work that makes for effective and satisfying educational experiences for online students. The joy of the educator is not just a perk. It is part of what fuels the educator's side of the student-instructor relationship, and it is a valuable motivator to keep going when challenges arise.

So, what are the inherent joys of online teaching? What motivates educators to seek opportunities in the online environment? Fortunately, so much about good online course design and teaching is inherently motivating. Certain aspects may appeal to some more than others, but in seeking to thrive, it is important to identify and cultivate what is motivating and joyful for you as an online educator.

The Joy of Flexibility

Practically speaking, the flexibility online education offers students is also attractive for many educators. A common remark about teaching online is how nice it must be to teach while wearing pajamas, but the advantages of online teaching extend far beyond comfortable apparel. Just like online students, the ability to work from home and to set our own schedules is attractive for many educators who are balancing other responsibilities and interests. Flexible schedules and the ability to work remotely are attractive to faculty with young families, those with older or sickly relatives in their care, those who live far from campus, those who wish to avoid wasting time in traffic congestion, those who teach as adjuncts in addition to their nonacademic primary career, those who must travel frequently, and those who may have health or mobility issues that make campus-based teaching challenging. At a basic level, the flexibility online teaching offers helps educators do more of what they want to with their lives outside of teaching.

The Joy of Creativity

Many faculty who teach online enjoy the creative aspects of developing an online course. Writing the course materials, designing the visuals, and crafting learning activities is inherently enjoyable work for many educators. Creating multimedia content can be downright exhilarating. Indeed, after completing course development, many educators feel a sense of pride and accomplishment akin to that of an artist or craftsperson completing a creative work such as a painting, woodwork, or textile art. When teaching the course, being able to witness students enjoying and appreciating your work of art is also deeply gratifying.

The Joy of Lifelong Learning

Many online educators derive excitement and happiness from the intellectual challenge of developing teaching and learning practices in a new digital space. Felten, Gardner, Schroeder, Lambert, and Barefoot (2016) state, "Effective institutions have practices and policies deliberately designed to foster learning by everyone on campus, recognizing that faculty and staff must continually learn so that they can help students to learn" (p. 5). Beyond professional development within an academic discipline, learning to teach online and continuing to identify teaching problems and finding innovative ways to solve them provide ample and rewarding learning opportunities to keep faculty engaged. Many find these sorts of challenges and the ability to overcome them immensely energizing. Like working a problem or solving a puzzle, the intellectual and creative challenges keep many online educators coming back for more. Although continued learning is important for all working in higher education today, it is especially important for those of us working in online education because the learning environment is so new and is rapidly changing how people interact.

Part of hitting our stride as online educators means including as part of our identity the role of lifelong learners who are perpetually curious and keenly aware that we are living in a time of great change and that there is always something new to learn. Embracing the vulnerable role of learner may not be aligned with how some initially envision hitting their strides. After all, when we imagine the lives of those we perceive as hitting their strides, we imagine confident competence, a consistently high level of performance, and a natural ease in the way they do their work. When we imagine these thriving people, sometimes we do not count ourselves among them because we know intimately our own confidence deficits, our own professional highs and lows, and our own struggles with our work. When we set stride-hitting goals for our future selves, we often hope for a time when our work will not feel so hard and when we will no longer struggle. Perhaps, though, hitting our strides means keeping ourselves in play between that space where we are so comfortable that we are stagnant and a space where we are lost, confused, and scared. Perhaps hitting our stride means embracing your role as a lifelong learner, answering the call to better learn so you might better teach.

Although all this learning requires effort, it is not depleting. By keeping our courses fresh, our students benefit, but we do too, partly because successfully inter-acting with students is inherently enjoyable and partly because we are keeping the experience of teaching our courses fresh and interesting for us as educators, the human beings on the other side of the student engage-ment equation. When this happens, we have hit our stride. We are not coasting. We have reached that optimal tension between speed and distance, exertion and endur-ance.

The Joy of Innovation

Furthermore, when we are engaged as online educators, we feel comfortable and confident in our abilities, so much so that we are willing to experiment and assume more risk. We celebrate and share our successes when we inno-vate and discover a new and effective teaching practice. Yet, we also have enough confidence in our professional selves to tolerate and recover from occasional failures. We are not devastated by mistakes; we learn from them and move on. We know that trying new things in our teaching work keeps the experience fresh and effective for students and also for ourselves.

Much innovation in online education involves the use of new educational technologies, and many edu-cators find appeal through experimenting with them. These educators tend to be early adopters who are first in line for the latest smartphone or tablet, with kitchens or garages full of gadgets and hobbies such as robotics, drones, science fiction, or fantasy. These educators are people who are eager to try the latest tools and to sign up for educational technology beta tests and pilot programs. Many educators find the technological aspect of online teaching so inherently enjoyable that they describe the work as play. Attend any educational technology training and you will hear someone say, "Let me *play* around with it and figure it out," or, "I'm looking forward to *playing* with this." The use of the joyful verb "play" in this context is not accidental; for many, learning to use a new technology is fun.

Invitation to Connect

Which aspects of online teaching give you joy as an educator? Share your thoughts on social media using #ThriveOnline.

WHEN TECHNOLOGY BECOMES INVISIBLE

Anyone who has learned how to drive a car has experienced the fading visibility of technology. When we first attempt to drive, we must be very intentional with every action. Knowing how firmly to press on the gas pedal and how far to turn the steering wheel require calculated and careful consideration. Maneuvering around immobile obstacles such as parked cars is nerve-racking, and merging with other traffic adds a layer of complexity that has made more than a few novice drivers break out in a sweat. Eventually, though, we gain more expertise and the mechanics of driving fade to the background. Instead of thinking about *how* to drive, we think about where we are going, we converse with passengers, we listen to the radio, and we enjoy the experience of driving in and of itself.

Many communication technologies have gone through a similar process of diminishing visibility. At some point in time, even a simple pencil was a new technology, and as we began to use it, we thought so much about the instrument that the thoughts we were trying to convey rivaled the thinking we needed to do to convey them. Typewriters, computers with word processors, and smartphones have gone through similar processes and have become more and more invisible to us with greater use.

Like new automobile drivers or those adopting new communication technologies, fledgling online educators often begin by feeling somewhat overwhelmed by the mechanics of the technology. Our concentration is wholly devoted to even the simplest teaching maneuvers, such as how to make an announcement or how to record a grade. With proper preparation, practice, and experience, however, the educational technologies we use for online teaching fade into the background. When online educators hit their strides, we recognize that good teaching is good teaching, regardless of the modality. The technology we use to build our online classrooms and to teach online becomes invisible, and we find that what remains is our students and ourselves.

KEY TAKEAWAYS FROM PART THREE

- Hitting your stride is not a sprint and is not a slow, meandering stroll. It is the optimized tension of speed and endurance. Professionally, this means seeking a certain level of challenge throughout your career.
- Online classes provide a unique opportunity for reflection, unlike teaching in other modalities. Educators can examine a previously taught class as they would a text, studying the content and interactions to assess their effectiveness.
- Online courses, when designed and facilitated well, provide three forms of interaction throughout the course: student-content, student-student, and student-instructor interaction. These interactions can take many forms but should be present in some way on a regular basis.
- Active learning requires meaningful action and reflection. Furthermore, reflection is more than one thing. Students need guidance and sometimes direct instruction about how to reflect.
- Online educators who thrive understand the properties of the Internet and their implications for online teaching, are aware of what they can do better online than they can face to face, and work to overcome the shortcomings of the online medium.

- With experience, educators can become as fluent and comfortable in the online classroom as they are in other teaching and learning spaces.
- Good teaching is good teaching, regardless of the modality.

TAKE ACTION TO THRIVE

New and experienced online educators and administrators can hit their strides. The following questions can help you reflect and take action to achieve a state of thriving in your career.

For Educators New to Online Teaching

- Examine your course for telltale signs of not hitting your stride as an online educator. Are your materials organized optimally for your students? Have you relied too heavily on text? Are your lectures too long, or are they recordings from an on-campus course? What changes can you make to improve your course? What resources will you need?
- Can you identify the three forms of interaction in your course: student-content, student-student, and student-instructor interaction?
- Do you know colleagues who appear to be hitting their stride in online teaching? Invite one for coffee or lunch. Ask about what works well for them in their online teaching. Ask what they most enjoy about teaching online.

For Online Educators Seeking to Grow

- In the active learning experiences in your course, have you provided students the opportunity and guidance they need to reflect on the learning experience? Have you defined for yourself and for your students what you mean by *reflection*, exactly? See Tables 3.1 and 3.2 for help in defining *reflection* for your class and your students.

- Have you maximized the learning experiences in your class to take full advantage of the diversity of your students in terms of their geographic location, cultural backgrounds, age, professional and life experience, and perspectives?

- Identify which aspects of online teaching bring you the most professional satisfaction. Are you taking full advantage of the opportunities to experience joy in your work?

For Administrators

- Reflect on the spoken or unspoken expectations for online education at your institution. Does a quality online educational experience mean replicating the on-campus experience identically? Or, is there room for online educators to leverage the unique opportunities the online medium provides?

- Does your institution provide what Felten and colleagues (2016) recommend: "practices and policies deliberately designed to foster learning by everyone on campus" (p. 5)?

PART FOUR

LEADING THE WAY

LEADING THE WAY

In higher education today, we have a large number of instructors who have come up through educational and cultural systems that revolve around the print medium, but we also have an emerging generation of students and, increasingly, educators who are coming up through educational and cultural systems that are digitally connected and networked. The landscape that is the setting for this cultural divide is an economically harsh one: Tuition rates have spiked, but wages for college graduates have been virtually stagnant. More students than ever before must balance school with work, yet debt for college loans continues to rise. Because of harsh economic realities, the constituencies served by higher education are shifting, and because of the information age, the ways people interact and communicate are evolving. Even traditional students who attend four-year institutions straight out of high school find it necessary to balance work and their educations. Perhaps not surprisingly, increasing numbers of these traditional students are at least occasionally opting for online courses, in many cases for the same reasons fully online students do: to help flex school schedules to allow time for work.

Interestingly, online education has a significant role to play in adapting higher education to these changes in the human experience. Through the relationships developed in the practice of online teaching, educators know students who are so committed to pursuing their degrees they are juggling more responsibilities and risking the investment of more personal resources than any preceding generation. Experience teaching online has made educators so comfortable with the technologies they use, they see past them to connect in real, human, and what have come to feel like natural ways with learners. Online educators, therefore, are perhaps best prepared and positioned to lead the way. For many, the opportunity to influence our home institutions and higher education more broadly is yet another way to thrive in our careers.

OPPORTUNITIES FOR LEADERSHIP

Depending on your role and your institutional context, opportunities for leadership will vary. Every institution is different and working in existing contexts to organically increase these opportunities will likely be more fruitful than trying to graft foreign ideas onto a native context.

Leadership is not confined to a position or title.

#ThriveOnline

To find leadership opportunities, you do not have to look very far.

The most important thing to know about leadership is that it is not confined to a position or title. To be a leader in online education, you do not need a title of provost, vice president, dean, or director. Leadership can, and should, be part of everyone's work. Kouzes and Posner (2007) stated, "Leadership is everyone's business. No matter what your position is, you have to take responsibility for the quality of leadership your constituents get. You—and that means all of us—are accountable for the leadership you demonstrate" (p. 339). For online educators, the most important constituents are students. Leadership is a significant component of the art of teaching. Other constituents might include colleagues from your department, fellow members of a committee, or your department head or dean. Leadership is not just top down on an organizational chart. We can lead from the sides or from below as Kouzes and Posner (2007) elaborate:

> Leadership development is self-development. Engineers have computers; painters, canvas and brushes; musicians, instruments. Leaders have only themselves. The instrument of leadership is the self, and mastery of the art of leadership comes from mastery of the self. Self-development is not about stuffing in a whole bunch of information or trying out the latest technique. It's about leading out of what is already in your soul. It's about liberating the leader within you. It's about setting yourself free. (p. 344)

To find leadership opportunities related to online education, you have to know yourself as an online educator. What are your strengths as an educator? What have you learned about online course development and teaching that might be helpful for others? Which values drive you to teach online? Which qualities are in your soul, ripe and ready to be liberated?

INVITATION TO REFLECT: DISCOVERING THE LEADER WITHIN

Freewriting is the practice of writing without stopping and without censoring or editing yourself for a specified length of time. Focused freewriting is similar to freewriting, but includes starting with a specific writing prompt. The goal of freewriting is quantity, not quality. Writers and creatives have used this method for decades to work through creative blocks and to push themselves to be more honest and authentic in their work. The most important part of freewriting is to keep your hand moving, as this is what will keep you from censoring and editing yourself. Freewriting should be done using paper and pen or pencil, not a computer.

Some of what you write when freewriting may not be very good or particularly meaningful. That's okay. Trust that the process of writing without stopping will help you uncover deeply held beliefs, thoughts, and values—an important part of discovering the leader within yourself. Following is a loose structure for freewriting:

- Set a timer for three minutes and write in long-hand starting with the following prompt: "What makes me passionate about teaching online is. . . ." When you are finished, do not go back and reread what you wrote.
- Stretch. Shake your hand loose. Relax quietly for a moment. After a short break, set the timer for another three minutes. Write in longhand starting with the following prompt: "The values that drive me to teach online are. . . ." When you are finished, do not go back and reread what you wrote.
- Set your pages aside. After at least a day, come back to your pages with a highlighter. Slowly read over your words. Highlight any phrases or short passages that resonate with you. These phrases and passages are the beginning of how you see yourself as an online educator. This is what is in your soul—the innate, unique, and essential parts of you with which you can lead.

Invitation to Connect: Sharing the Leader Within
If you are comfortable doing so, share with the #ThriveOnline community what you have discovered about the leader within you.

Online educators must work to make our students more visible.

#ThriveOnline

PUTTING LEADERSHIP IN ACTION

Soul-searching self-reflection is important and should be practiced on a somewhat regular basis. However, reflection alone does not a leader make. It is also important to take action. As online educators, what kinds of actions can we take to demonstrate and practice leadership?

Helping Our Students Be Seen

At the very least, every online educator must work to make students more visible. Everyone, regardless of role or institution, can share their teaching stories and help colleagues in online education tell theirs. We need to tell stories of the students we are able to reach because we are teaching online asynchronous classes. When we have a student who gives birth midsemester and still successfully completes the course, we need to tell that story. When we have a military student who submits an exam while serving on active duty halfway around the world, we need to tell that story. When we have students who are working full time, raising families, and who are participating in our courses into the wee hours to meet class deadlines, we have an obligation to share those stories.

We cannot allow online students to remain invisible on our campuses, for they are just as present and just as important as the 18- to 22-year-old students who are sitting in campus lecture halls and playing Frisbee on the quad.

Invitation to Connect

What have your students juggled, sacrificed, or over-come in pursuit of their education in your online classes? Share the stories that inspire you to do the work you do. Be sure to preserve student privacy in ways that are nonidentifying with the #ThriveOnline community.

Sharing Our Work

Another way to lead as an online educator is to share your online course development and teaching work, such as through teaching and learning showcases in your institution. Share your approaches with active student-centered learning. Share your experiments with new or new-to-you academic technologies and online teaching approaches. Sharing online teaching experiences is an important and effective strategy in building institutional literacy on the needs of online students as well as online course design and teaching. Exposure to a variety of approaches in a range of disciplines can help fellow educators and administrators understand more about how online education works, help demonstrate that online education can work in a wide range of disciplines for a wide range of students, and help create a more digitally literate institution.

Submitting proposals at online teaching and learning conferences as well as at general conferences in your discipline is an effective strategy in providing leadership as well. Changing the conversation about online teaching in your discipline can begin in your home academic department, but to become firmly established it needs to gain a strong foothold throughout your discipline. Making presentations at discipline-specific conferences is one way to show that online teaching is being done and being done well within your field. The strategies discussed in Part One of this book regarding how to change the conversation about the value of online education in our home institutions can also be applied when we network with other colleagues at summits and conferences.

Communicating the Complexities

As you find opportunities to share your experiences with online course development and teaching, it will be important to educate colleagues and administrators about how development and facilitation of online courses are two distinct, necessary, and demanding aspects of online education. Misunderstanding the complexities involved in delivering quality online educational experiences, specifically about the need to separate development and facilitation work, are at the root of many inequities for online education professionals and are often the cause of quality issues in online courses.

Traditional higher education typically conflates development and facilitation of face-to-face courses into one effort, and for good reason. This approach in face-to-face teaching is effective and economical. As a result, though, faculty developing and teaching online courses experience significant tension with support structures, faculty development approaches, student success initiatives, promotion and tenure processes, and work assignments that have been organized around a method of teaching that compresses development and facilitation into one effort.

Helping others understand the rigorous demands of online course development and teaching can be an important first step in creating an environment more inclusive of online education and educators and in creating institutions that better serve online students.

Representation in Institutional Governance and Service Committees

Becoming active in your institution's governance as an advocate for online teaching and learning is another way to serve as an online education leader and change agent. Governance systems, policies, and issues manifest themselves differently at different institutions, but there are opportunities to get involved to ensure that online education is included and considered by your college or university.

One way to be involved is to participate in curriculum committees in your academic department. Be engaged in curriculum development and revision to resist segregation according to modality and resultant bifurcations of curricula, which when allowed to deepen can lead to unpleasant conflict among instructors and administrators, the need for significant reworking of curricula and course designs, accreditation problems, inequitable evaluations of teaching, and problems with student success such as when students in an on-campus section are exposed to a curriculum different from those in the same course offered online.

Another way to get involved in governance is to attend faculty senate meetings, become a member of your senate or governing body, or attend public board meetings. As issues and discussions arise, share your perspective as an experienced online educator. Of course, participate in committees about online education, but in the absence of those, seek committees, events, work groups, and task forces relating to academic technologies; learning management systems; multimedia development; innovation; and faculty development, training, and support, all of which frequently intersect with the world of online education and all of which are in need of representation from online educators.

Leadership Through Policy Work

Another perhaps less obvious way to be an online education leader at your institution is to examine institutional policies about academic integrity, student conduct, equity and inclusion, and student life. Determine if these policies adequately address the needs of your online students.

INVITATION TO REFLECT: YOUR SERVICE CONTRIBUTIONS

1. At your institution, which committees, events, work groups, task forces, or other service areas might value your expert contributions the most? Where is your service needed most?
2. Alternatively, which committees, events, work groups, task forces, or other service areas might you learn the most from?

For example, if your institution's student conduct code addresses behavioral problems such as disrupting classes with noise or distracting and inappropriate behavior that impinges on the rights of other students to engage fully in their educations, find out if it also addresses the disruption of online courses by the use of aggressive, harassing, or abusive language in online communications such as discussion boards. Although these may not be audible contemporaneous disturbances, these kinds of behaviors can still be disruptive and can detract from the educational experience of others in the online class. Other institutional policies can be campus centric as well and can ignore the experiences of online students. If necessary, work to make these policies more inclusive of online students.

Institutional policies that relate to faculty, such as intellectual property ownership, evaluation of teaching, and promotion and tenure policies and procedures, can likewise exclude the online education experience. Determine if these policies and procedures adequately address the needs of faculty working in online education. If necessary, advocate to make these policies and procedures more inclusive of online educators. Take heed, though; these will not be easy conversations and will likely include much more complex solutions than simply extending existing campus-based policies online.

Intellectual Property
The question of intellectual property, for instance, can be much more straightforward on campus. The teaching materials used in on-campus teaching are mere supplements for the actual teaching work, which is conducted

mostly through speech. Online, however, most of the course is written or recorded in some way and as such constitutes a text that can at least potentially be used by other faculty members or in other ways. The question of intellectual property of such materials is far more complex. Is the written course considered work for hire and owned by the institution? Can the institution take that intellectual property and use it in other ways, such as in fee-based self-paced courses that do not require facilitation? Can the institution use video of a faculty member for other purposes or in other courses without that faculty member's express permission? Can a copy of an online course be used as a master course? If so, how much of the course can be used? How much can be changed?

What if a faculty member leaves the institution? Can the faculty member's likeness and course materials continue to be used without continual compensation? Or is the written and recorded online course entirely the property of the faculty member? What if a faculty member dies? How does ownership of the digital materials transfer? Are the faculty members' heirs entitled to continued royalties?

If the faculty members own the materials, can they offer the written and recorded online courses at other competing institutions or is the ownership of the intellectual property somewhere in between?

These are policy questions each institution must grapple with and require leaders who understand not only the nature of online education but also how online courses are produced, archived, and replicated at their institution.

Including Online Education Equitably in the Assessment of Teaching

The question of how teaching is assessed is another policy area in need of leadership from those with experience in the online environment. A few areas to probe at your institution might include the following:

- Does your institution use a standard set of questions for student evaluation of instruction? Do those questions pertain to different instructional modalities?
- Does your institution use a standard set of criteria for the administrative evaluation of instruction? Do the criteria adequately address the demands of course design for online components of courses as well as facilitation in various modalities?
- Do program assessments include criteria and evidence from all modalities of instruction used in the program?
- Is the use of educational technology treated as essential and expected across modalities, or is it optional?

In evaluating online teaching, administrators can err in both directions by essentially ignoring or excessively scrutinizing the delivery of online education. On campus, the standard practice is for educators to have one teaching observation by a supervisor of one class meeting per year, although sometimes these on-campus evaluations happen even less frequently. By contrast, in some places, online teaching is scrutinized in ways that many faculty believe are unfair and impinge on academic freedom. In some institutions, such as several for-profit institutions, evaluation of online teaching requires a certain ratio of instructor discussion posts per student contributions or a measurement of response times to posted questions, which are standards that may or may not capture the quality of the educational experience and level of student engagement but are used because they are quickly and straightforwardly measured. Perhaps because evaluators do not know what evidence to look for that constitutes good online teaching, they look for the evidence that is most apparent and easiest to count, even though this may not be the most significant data in terms of student-faculty engagement or student success.

Barriers do exist that make evaluation of online teaching difficult to accomplish, such as difficulties in getting a supervisor digital access to courses taught by others. Because of differences in how registration and enrollment systems work with learning management systems, and because of institutional policies, simply adding a supervisor to the roster of an online course can be challenging, especially when faculty and administrators do not understand how registration, enrollment, and learning management systems operate or system administrators do not understand the need for evaluation and feedback to improve teaching and learning.

In other places, access does not pose as much of a problem, but supervisors who do not understand online education are put in a position of being responsible for evaluating online course design and teaching despite their lack of experience with online education. Although challenging to imagine, this practice is akin to asking someone to evaluate an on-campus educator's performance if the evaluator has never even been a student in an on-campus class. Yet in many places, this is what online educators face. Supervisors must evaluate online teaching, but they may not have even a basic understanding of the kinds of evidence for which to look.

Invitation to Connect

Imagine you had the power to determine the criteria for the evaluation of your online teaching. What are the three most important aspects you would like to have considered? Share your thoughts with the #ThriveOnline community.

Including Online Education for Consideration in Promotion and Tenure

The need for online course design and teaching evaluation is especially problematic and high stakes when an online educator is applying for promotion and tenure. Those responsible for reviewing the educator's qualifications in teaching will have discipline-specific expertise but may not know the first thing about online course design or teaching and may even have biases against online education. (Indeed, if the reports discussed in Part One of this book are accurate, they are statistically likely to have biases against online education.) In this circumstance, online educators and their evaluators may find it helpful to have an objective and neutral set of standards for online course design and facilitation that the reviewer can at least refer to in conducting the evaluation. Ideally, the standards used will be research based and adopted by an entire department, program, college, or institution.

However, in some cases, online educators may be up for tenure or promotion in an institution that has not yet adopted or developed these metrics for online teaching. Providing leadership in this context might begin with developing a rubric or set of criteria to assess online course design and teaching. In a department or institution whose faculty have little experience with online education, an online course developer and educator might submit a course for review in the tenure and promotion process along with an overview of design and facilitation criteria used in developing and teaching a course. Such a presentation would demonstrate a research and evidence-based approach to online teaching as well as provide useful documentation of the educator's reflections about the qualities and standards that constitute sound, effective online course design and teaching. Such documented criteria can help to develop important literacy about online education for individuals and for departments, programs, institutions, and disciplines and can improve the accuracy and fairness of teaching evaluations for online educators. Collaboratively creating these resources with other experienced online educators at your institution can make them more valuable and can accelerate adoption.

Another way to build institutional literacy around the evaluation of online course design and teaching is to implement peer observations, online educator to online educator. This can be done in house, informally or formally, and can be accomplished through the use of internally developed or externally developed criteria and processes such as those available from the Quality Matters or Online Learning Consortium organizations, or from other institutions that have developed their own internal criteria and made them publicly available. Informed assessments of online course design and teaching will provide richer, more useful feedback for online educators, and reports of these assessments will serve to improve literacy about online education at administrative levels.

As we develop or adopt these practices, procedures, and policies, we are institutionalizing online teaching and learning. We are leading online education into the mainstream of higher education.

FOR THOSE IN LEADERSHIP ROLES

Although leadership can and should come from every online educator regardless of title or position, for those who do hold formal leadership positions, understanding what online educators really need to thrive in their work is crucial. When asked about the proper role of leaders and administrators in supporting online educators, Thomas Cavanagh, associate vice president of the Center for Distributed Learning at the University of Central Florida, stated, "If an institution knows why it is pursuing an online learning agenda, and provides the proper support to accomplish those goals, adoption and acceptance should be a natural outcome of the process" (T. Cavanagh, personal communication, April 27, 2017). Understanding

INVITATION TO REFLECT: POLICY WORK AT YOUR INSTITUTION

1. Policy work is possible in the areas of curriculum development and approval, the evaluation of teaching, intellectual property ownership, and promotion and tenure as a means of providing leadership for online education, educators, and students, among others. Which areas have you encountered at your home institution that might benefit from better representation of online education in departmental or institutional policy?

2. Have you or colleagues who teach online or your online students ever felt underrepresented by one of your institution's policies? What revisions would be necessary to make them more inclusive? Would the changes be fairly straightforward, or would significant reconsideration be necessary?

the larger context of your institutional online learning agenda and communicating that context with online educators is an important first step. More practically, the following sections comprise an annotated list of what online educators need most.

A Reliable Learning Management System With Technical Support

Some have predicted the death of the learning management system, suggesting that educational technology is diversifying and that many tools can be used to disperse educational content at a lower cost. Although there are many ways to create and distribute content, the learning management system remains a central gathering place for students in a course, program, or institution; the most convenient means of recording and communicating assessment of student work; and the most effective approach to ensuring student privacy. Having and maintaining a working system is equivalent to providing a safe building on campus. Online educators and students need a working classroom, and they need technical support for when something goes wrong.

Time

Many believe that financial support is high on the list of what online educators need. Funding is important, but even in institutions with well-funded online education initiatives, the factor of greatest scarcity is instructor time. Educators need two distinct blocks of time, one devoted to the development of the online course and one devoted to teaching the online course. On-campus development and teaching can be conflated, but online they cannot. Online educators need the resource of time to create and deliver effective online courses.

Instructional Design Services

The field of instructional design is complex, and the roles and responsibilities of instructional designers vary greatly depending on their industry and their level of education. Corporate training needs, structures, and approaches differ from those used in K–12 settings. Even in higher education institutions, the roles of instructional designers vary depending on the institution's other available resources. For example, in smaller institutions, it is not unusual to have one instructional designer who serves as a one-stop shop for design, technical support, media development, and faculty training. In larger organizations, the instructional design and related roles can be more specialized.

Generally, in higher education, instructional designers are professionals who partner with faculty members to design and create effective online learning experiences for students. Instructional designers are knowledgeable about educational theory, pedagogy, communication, online course design and delivery, and educational technologies, and they work with faculty members to create online courses. The availability of instructional design services is essential, especially if the institution's mission is to ramp up online offerings with any speed or attention to quality.

Without instructional design services, instructors themselves need to become experts in these specialty areas. Online education requires a much more collaborative approach than traditional face-to-face teaching. Providing instructors with access to instructional designers is essential.

Media Development Services

Academic leaders should also be aware that online educators need media development services. The creation of multimedia for online courses is important for several reasons. It makes the best use of the online medium, it

Instructional designers are professionals who partner with faculty members to design and create effective online learning experiences for students.

#ThriveOnline

helps engage students and meet their expectations for the online learning environment, and it helps establish a strong sense of instructor presence in the class better than text alone. Depending on the types of online programs an institution offers, and the degree to which institutions are reliant on publisher-provided media materials, different levels of media development services will be needed. Larger institutions with scientific and technical academic programming may find it necessary to invest in media developers specializing in animation, custom programming, and videography. However, simply providing access to media equipment, studio space with good lighting and acoustics, software, and the necessary training to use these resources can also be extremely helpful for instructors who often are wholly unfamiliar with media production.

Analytics and Assessment

For institutions committed to producing the highest quality online education, providing online educators with access to analytics and assessment tools, as well as support in using them, is necessary to develop and hone effective online teaching methods. One of the greatest advantages of online education is the ability to collect data about how students interact with content, each other, and educators, and to which degrees these interactions actually assist with learning.

Online education is a relatively new field, which means additional research and development will be needed for some time. Data analytics, assessment tools, and support will help accelerate our understanding of which strategies are effective.

Time and Resources for Continual Improvement

Partly because online education is such a new field, and partly because educational technologies and the devices we use to access them are rapidly evolving, providing online educators with work flows that include time and resources for the periodic redevelopment of online courses is critical for providing quality online educational experiences. Courses should be redeveloped routinely. Some factors that will require greater frequency of redevelopment are the nature of the content (i.e., rapidly changing fields like computer science), the number of students taking the specific course (greater numbers argue for more frequent redevelopment to help prevent academic integrity violations), and emerging technologies and pedagogical approaches that may provide significant improvements to the learning experiences of students.

Inclusion of Online Education Efforts in the Tenure and Promotion Process

Higher education leaders who wish to support online educators and expand online education initiatives in their institutions should work to recognize the effort and expertise needed for online course development and teaching in the promotion and tenure process. Ariel Anbar, director of Arizona State University's Center for Education Through eXploration, advises administrators and leaders to make "the *moral* case" to promote online education (A. Anbar, personal communication, June 4, 2017). When asked about the role of leaders in online education, Anbar recommended approaching online education leadership "as a way to improve *the overall average quality* of learning" and "to pair a push for online excellence with a push for teaching-and-learning excellence through better assessment processes *for the benefit of* students" (personal communication, June 4, 2017). To demonstrate commitment to this moral pursuit, Anbar recommends "modifying tenure and promotion policies so that the effort is valued" (A. Anbar, personal communication, June 4, 2017).

If leadership values online education as part of the institutional mission, efforts and achievements in providing quality online educational experiences should be included in the assessment of faculty work.

Training

Finally, instructors who are making the transition from traditional brick-and-mortar teaching to online teaching need access to efficient, high-quality training. Interestingly, for many of the same reasons students seek online learning opportunities, convenience and flexibility being chief among them, one of the most efficient ways to deliver instructor training is online. Training for online educators is needed in several areas: pedagogy, online course design and development, online course facilitation, and educational technologies. Providing access to a learning management system is not sufficient. Online education is complex, and training is needed if it is to be done well.

ROLE OF FACULTY DEVELOPMENT IN ACHIEVING DIGITAL FLUENCY

To meet the needs of tomorrow's students, higher education institutions will need to improve digital literacy among instructors and staff but ultimately go beyond mere literacy to achieve digital fluency. When we are fluent in the technologies we use, they recede from view so that we are better able to focus on the people they are meant to serve. The goal is not to master the technology for its own sake, but rather to better connect the people who are using it. Everyone working in online education today has a role in leading the way to meet this goal. As more instructors achieve digital fluency and experience the human connections that can be made with technological assistance, less attention will be paid to the technologies we use, and we can focus more on the students we are serving.

Significant professional development will be necessary to help educators develop digital fluency. Yet we know that in many places instructors are challenged to complete professional development because of time and other constraints. Felten and colleagues (2016) discuss a need to prioritize learning for instructors and staff as well as for students. They note that attitudes toward faculty development are based in institutional culture and remark that some institutions operate with a "narrative of constraint," where "faculty development [is] something done to hostile or disengaged faculty" (Felten et al., 2016, p. 40). In such institutions, faculty are too busy and too overworked for development. When development work is required, faculty participate grudgingly and minimally and are not fully engaged. Instead, Felton and colleagues (2016) envision a "narrative of growth," which "leads to faculty development initiatives emerging from the professional goals and habits of a busy faculty who willingly seek the expertise and perspectives of peers" (p. 40).

In these healthy organizations, faculty's ethos is a desire to thrive, to challenge themselves to grow and feel vitality and engagement in their work. Felten and colleagues (2016) call for this willingness to grow as a precursor to thriving in our work:

> Just as we work to help our students become more engaged and resilient learners, we must cultivate our colleagues and institutions as *learners with the potential to grow and thrive*. This may require significant changes for individuals and organizations as we transform into learning-centered institutions. (p. 42, emphasis added)

Those who wish to provide leadership in online education can resist espousing narratives of constraint and can contribute to the narrative of growth at their home institutions. Such attitudinal shifts are more effective when they come from the ground up and are then supported and celebrated from the top.

Interestingly, in Beach, Sorcinelli, Austin, and Rivard's (2016) study of faculty development leaders in the United States and Canada, the need for faculty development about online education in particular is well documented.

Higher education needs to go beyond digital literacy to achieve digital fluency.

#ThriveOnline

Beach and colleagues (2016) report findings that show teaching in online and distance environments is one of the top two issues the field of faculty development should address in the next five years, second only to assessment of student learning outcomes. They attribute the need for faculty development in online learning to the increase of online educational programming and resultant changing roles of faculty members:

> Since 2006 the landscape of faculty roles and institutional imperatives has broadened considerably. We have seen the array of technologies that have an impact on faculty work expand at astonishing rates (e.g., technologies to facilitate teaching and learning, platforms for virtual scholarly collaboration, and avenues for general communication). Online degrees have increased in number at traditional brick-and-mortar institutions, often challenging and shifting the teaching practices of faculty not previously trained or interested in teaching online. (Beach et al., 2016, p. 134)

Beach and colleagues' study (2016) identifies a shift from the age of networked faculty development to one that expands the networked approach to include assessment so that evidence might be used to inform faculty development programming, institutional priorities, and student success initiatives. With the exception of e-mail delivered through systems external to the learning management system and phone calls or text messages, online courses record virtually all interactions in the online classroom space. An archived online course is a rich text that can be carefully analyzed and studied at the researcher's or assessor's convenience. To capture a face-to-face course similarly would require elaborate video recording, transcribing (sometimes of simultaneous conversations), and digitizing written assignments and class work, which could only be accomplished at great cost and inconvenience. Significantly, therefore, online courses may be better suited than traditional classes for documenting the evidence that will be needed to inform tomorrow's institutional direction and decisions.

Interestingly, researchers found that faculty development was not the work of one department in an institution and called instead for a collaborative, institution-wide approach to faculty development, including departments ranging from graduate schools to student health and counseling centers as "potential allies who can contribute to faculty development initiatives" (Beach et al., 2016, p. 144). Institution-wide commitments are necessary to meet the needs of today's complex students and to overcome the challenges ahead. Digital literacy and fluency are lofty goals and require broad collaboration to achieve.

Transformational Faculty Development Needed for the Work Ahead

Accomplishing the goals of making institutions more inclusive of online education and helping instructors achieve digital fluency requires faculty development that goes beyond mere technology training, individual improvements to teaching and learning, and support for tenure and promotion. Faculty development that is transformational for the institution is needed for not only achieving the institution's missions and goals but also establishing what the mission and goals are in the first place. Schroeder (2011) argues that the appropriate role for faculty development units in institutions of higher learning is at the center of the institution, helping to shape its mission and goals and helping to prepare and organize faculty to achieve them, a role with a much further reach than individual faculty development.

When faculty development units are properly resourced and situated at an institution, they can be powerful agencies for change. A healthy faculty development unit runs horizontally, across faculty teaching in all modalities, and vertically, helping to connect leadership's vision with student success. Such an organization is a complex web of relationships and activity, a hub that connects administration, faculty, and students. In institutions with lofty goals such as trying to help faculty gain digital fluency to help students succeed in a networked world, a robust faculty development organization can be a powerful and transformative force.

Online Education Leadership

Although improving attitudes toward online education and educators is wholly worthwhile on its own, the significance and impact of this work will certainly not stop at the lecture hall door. Students are digitally connected whether they are taking online courses, on-campus courses, or a mixture of both. Their communication habits, their usability expectations, and the very ways they think are changing. Those changes do not manifest themselves only in online courses, and therefore online educators and leaders who support them are likely to have many more impacts than online courses alone.

In today's complex higher education environment, there is an immense need for wise and effective leadership in general, but there is a specific need for such leaders to emerge from within the online education community. If we are to integrate online education and educators into traditional higher education, we need leaders who understand the specific demands of online education and the unique needs of online educators and students. Actions all online educators can take to provide leadership include allowing their work and the students they serve to be known in conversations about online education, mentoring colleagues, participating and leading faculty development initiatives, participating in educational technology pilot programs, participating in institutional governance, and advocating for structures that support online educators. Consideration should be given to the risk level associated with these various leadership activities. Especially in governance and advocacy realms, risks to employment status can be uncomfortably high, especially for part-time, adjunct, and untenured faculty. Educators in these high-risk groups may wish to participate in less controversial arenas. Educators in lower risk groups may therefore bear a greater responsibility to participate in arenas that are more hotly contested.

Leadership Qualities Needed at All Levels

In a study of more than 75,000 international respondents, repeated 4 times over the course of 20 years, Kouzes and Posner (2007) found 4 traits respondents identified as necessary in leaders: being honest, forward looking, inspiring, and competent. For leaders in online education at all levels, it is not difficult to imagine how these characteristics might be embodied.

Leaders in higher education need to be honest, Kouzes and Posner's (2007) first indispensable leadership trait, in portraying the efficacy of online education in general terms, as well as in acknowledging specific strengths and weaknesses in delivering online education at their own institutions. Leaders also should be honest in recognizing the demands placed on faculty who are practicing online education in a system designed for campus-based instruction. Honest leadership would also acknowledge the need for collegiality among faculty, regardless of primary teaching modality and rank. Such collegiality cuts both ways, providing more inclusivity for online educators and more empathy and support for traditional educators who are fearful or intimidated by the need to become more digitally fluent.

Leaders today also need to be forward thinking, Kouzes and Posner's (2007) second indispensable leadership trait, to anticipate the needs of today's students in tomorrow's workplaces. An eye to the future is also helpful in predicting how the ways we communicate digitally will continue to be adapted by those of us working in higher education, regardless of our teaching modalities. How will adaptive and personalized learning have an impact on online and traditional classrooms? How might media such as virtual reality be used to create transformative educational experiences? How might augmented reality help students bring their studies into their lives and vice versa? How will artificial intelligence agents, such as the artificial, nonhuman teaching assistant Jill Watson used in a course offered at the Georgia Institute of Technology (Lipko, 2016), change the ways we support faculty and students?

INVITATION TO REFLECT: ARTIFICIAL INTELLIGENCE

1. How might you be able to use artificial intelligence to support your teaching?
2. How do you imagine your students would respond to help from an artificial intelligence robot?
3. What do you imagine are the ethical implications of using artificial intelligence in teaching and learning?

The ability to inspire others is Kouzes and Posner's (2007) third indispensable leadership trait, necessary for bringing skeptics and critics to adopt new ways of thinking about teaching and learning. Inspiration is also essential to effect institutional change and to persuade colleagues to leave the comfortable, known ways of doing things to

Invitation to Connect

Share your predictions about the role of artificial intelligence in higher education with the #ThriveOnline community.

try innovative approaches that may or may not succeed. The ability to inspire is also crucial in transforming cultures of scarcity to cultures of growth, as these perspectives are so much a matter of attitude.

Finally, the fourth of Kouzes and Posner's (2007) top leadership traits, competence, is needed to deeply understand the complexities of developing and facilitating online courses and programs. Large high-quality online education providers invest significantly in professionals with specialized expertise to develop and maintain online programs. Institutions with smaller staffs on smaller budgets must still meet the same competencies, if in more economical ways. No one leader will possess every required competency, but leaders should understand which competencies are needed collectively.

Leadership to #ThriveOnline

In addition to Kouzes and Posner's (2007) top four leadership traits, in the context of higher education today, leaders should also appreciate their unique place in historical context. This trait relates somewhat to the concept of being forward looking, but it also requires leaders to appreciate the magnitude of change they are experiencing as well as how rare such changes are in the course of history. The information age and the rise of Internet access has created a new, digital dimension of human connection. Virtually every sphere of humanity has been affected— politics and government, commerce, agriculture, health, transportation, and popular culture, to name but a few. Even metaphysical concerns such as what constitutes fact

and truth have been affected in what some are now calling the post-truth era. Higher education is not immune
to these changes, though some may wish it were so. We
are no longer simply charged with improving teaching
and learning or with reforming higher education. We are
charged with reimagining and reinventing it altogether.
For this work, we need honest, forward-looking, inspiring,
and competent leaders. However, we also need leaders
who understand that the world is in the midst of an evolutionary leap and that the responsibility of leadership in
such a time is great.

The true and proper role of leaders in such a context may not be to propose solutions for the problems in
higher education, but rather to engage in true, collaborative academic inquiry. After all, the information age is
really just getting started; we cannot yet fathom how it
will end or where it will take us. Felton and colleagues
(2016) explored the role of leadership in creating campus
culture, and, interestingly, it directly relates to thriving:

> Campus cultures are like organisms that must be
> carefully tended to stay healthy *and thrive*. When
> the simple question, what is best for students
> and their learning? frames decision making at an
> institution, a reinforcing cycle develops to ensure
> that learning will be a central priority across
> campus. Indeed, inquiry is an essential leader-
> ship tool in the academy, and effective leaders at
> any level typically are more likely to pose critical
> questions than dictate what must happen. (p. 145,
> emphasis added)

Perhaps the best thing we can do as online educators and leaders in this time of profound change is to engage in true and genuine inquiry.

This means asking the difficult questions, exploring even when we do not know exactly where we will end up, and experimenting even knowing that our experiments may fail. It means questioning the ways we have always done things and being courageous enough to ask if there a better way. We are in the midst of an evolutionary leap forward. Our roles as online educators and online education leaders is to innovate in this time and space. Indeed, it is difficult these days to avoid the call for innovation in higher education literature, blogs, conferences, and discussions. The buzz about innovation is exciting, but too often innovation focuses on technology and immediate problem-solving. These are important and are certainly important parts of the overall picture. However, inquiry is larger than innovation.

Genuine inquiry does not already have an answer, which means it requires tremendous courage. Genuine inquiry asks the big questions such as, "Do the old ways still hold? How might we be different? How does our new digital connectedness change education and the humanity it serves? How might it do so?" These questions require boundless imagination as well as immense courage to pursue. This is the work of online educators. This is work we can be proud of. This is work in which we can thrive.

KEY TAKEAWAYS FROM PART FOUR

- Because student demographics are changing and increasing numbers of nontraditional students are seeking college educations, and because of the influence of the Internet on how people communicate and learn, online educators are uniquely prepared and positioned for leadership within higher education.
- To lead with authenticity, we must develop and know ourselves and lead from our core values and strengths.
- Opportunities for leadership are plentiful and varied and can be found in teaching work, service work, policy work—in every role, regardless of title.
- Research shows that four characteristics are perceived as being necessary in leaders: being honest, forward looking, inspiring, and competent (Kouzes and Posner, 2007).
- Problem-solving and innovation are important aspects of leadership, but more open-ended academic inquiry also plays a key role.

TAKE ACTION TO THRIVE

Leadership is possible for new online educators, for those with more experience, and for higher education administrators. The following reflections and actions will hopefully help you find opportunities for leadership that will help you—and others—thrive in the field of online education.

For Educators New to Online Teaching

- Identify opportunities to make your online students, their struggles, and their achievements visible at your institution.
- Explore opportunities at your institution for you to share the perspectives of online students and educators, such as in curriculum committees, academic technology committees, and elsewhere.

For Online Educators Seeking to Grow

- If your department or institution does not already have peer mentoring or online teaching assessment guidelines, work with colleagues to create them and advocate for their use.
- Reflect on your core values and strengths. Seek leadership opportunities that build on these aspects of yourself. Embracing authentic leadership opportunities can help you thrive as an online education leader.

For Administrators

- Assess the degree to which your institution's resources are used to support online education. How can you better leverage your institution's strengths? How can you improve weaker areas?
- Assess faculty development initiatives at your campus. How well do they support online educators?

Are your faculty development initiatives and personnel well connected horizontally and vertically? Are they limited to training, or are they more transformative in nature?

- Is your institution guided by the simple question of what is best for students and their learning?
- In addition to innovation and problem-solving in relation to online education, is your institution engaged in genuine academic inquiry?

REFERENCES

Adams Becker, S., Brown, M., Dahlstrom, E., Davis, A., DePaul, K., Diaz, V., & Pomerantz, J. (2018). *The New Media Consortium Horizon Report: 2018 Higher Education Edition.* Available from https://library.educause.edu/~/media/files/library/2018/8/2018horizonreport.pdf

Allen, E., Seaman, J., Poulin, R., & Straut, T. (2016). *Online report card: Tracking online education in the United States.* Available from http://onlinelearningsurvey.com/reports/onlinereportcard.pdf

Beach, A., Sorcinelli, M. D., Austin, A., & Rivard, J. (2016). *Faculty development in the age of evidence: Current practices, future imperatives.* Sterling, VA: Stylus.

Bloom, B. S. (1956). *Taxonomy of educational objectives, handbook I: The cognitive domain.* New York, NY: David McKay.

Bryan, M., Cameron, J., & Allen, C. (1998). *The artist's way at work: Riding the dragon.* New York, NY: William Morrow.

California State University, Chico. (2016). *The rubric.* Available from https://www.csuchico.edu/eoi/

Cameron, J. (2002). *The artist's way.* New York, NY: Penguin.

Carnevale, A., Smith, N., Melton, M., & Price, E. (2015). *Learning while earning: The new normal.* Available from https://cew.georgetown.edu/wp-content/uploads/Working-Learners-Report.pdf

Delen, E., Liew, J., & Willson, V. (2014). Effects of interactivity and instructional scaffolding on learning: Self-regulation in online video-based environments. *Computers and Education 78*, 312–320. doi:10.1016/j.compedu.2014.06.018

Everson, M. (2009). *Understanding the instructor's role in facilitating online discussions.* Available from http://www .facultyfocus.com/articles/online-education/understanding -the-instructors-role-in-facilitating-online-discussions/

Feldstein, M. & Hill, P. (2016). *Personalized learning: What it really is and why it really matters.* Available from http://er .educause.edu/articles/2016/3/personalized-learning-what-it-really-is-and-why-it-really-matters

Felten, P., Gardner, J., Schroeder, C., Lambert, L., & Barefoot, B. (2016). *The undergraduate experience: Focusing institutions on what matters most.* San Francisco, CA: Jossey-Bass.

Fink, D. L. (2003). *Creating significant learning experiences: An integrated approach to designing college courses.* San Francisco, CA: Wiley.

Gao, F., Zhang, T. & Franklin, T. (2013). Designing asynchronous online discussion environments: Recent progress and possible future directions. *British Journal of Educational Technology, 44*(3), 469–483. doi:10.1111/j.1467-8535.2012.01330.x

Grossman, R. (2009). Structures for facilitating student reflection. *College Teaching, 57*(1), 15–22. doi:10.3200/ctch.57.1.15-22

Hibbert, M. (2014). *What makes an online instructional video compelling?* Available from http://er.educause.edu/articles/2014/4/what-makes-an-online-instructional-video-compelling

Higher Learning Advocates. (2017). *Building a new system of higher learning.* Available from https://docs.wixstatic.com/ugd/48a79d_a154565d69474c949b9d2b49ede78677.pdf

Kennepohl, D. K. (2016). *Teaching science online: Practical guidance for effective instruction and lab work.* Sterling, VA: Stylus.

Kouzes, J., & Posner, B. (2007). *The leadership challenge* (4th ed.). San Francisco, CA: Jossey-Bass.

Kuh, G. (2008). *High-impact practices: What they are, who has access to them, and why they matter.* Available from https://www.aacu.org/leap/hips

Lipko, H. (2016). *Meet Jill Watson: Georgia Tech's first AI teaching assistant.* Retrieved from https://pe.gatech.edu/blog/meet-jill-watson-georgia-techs-first-ai-teaching-assistant

Michael, J. (2006). Where's the evidence that active learning works? *Advance in Physiology Education, 30*(4), 159–167. doi:10.1152/advan.00053.2006

Moore, M. (1989). Editorial: Three types of interaction. *American Journal of Distance Education, 3*(2), 1–2. doi:10.1080/08923648909526659

Online Learning Consortium. (2014). *OLC quality scorecard.* Available from https://onlinelearningconsortium.org/consult/quality-scorecard/

Perry, W. (1999). *Forms of ethical and intellectual development in the college years: A scheme.* San Francisco, CA: Jossey-Bass.

Prince, M. (2004). Does active learning work? A review of the research. *Journal of Engineering Education, 93*(3), 223–231.

Purdue University. (2018). Using research and evidence. *Purdue University Online Writing Lab.* Available from https://owl.purdue.edu/owl/general_writing/academic_writing/establishing_arguments/research_and_evidence.html

Quality Matters. (2018). *Higher education rubric workbook: Standards for course design* (6th ed.). Available from https://www.qualitymatters.org/sites/default/files/PDFs/StandardsfromtheQMHigherEducationRubric.pdf

Riggs, S., & Linder, K. (2016). *Actively engaging students in online asynchronous classes.* Manhattan, KS: IDEA Center.

Robertson, R. J., & Riggs, S. (2017). Collaborative learning in online, asynchronous classes. In K. Linder & C. Hayes (Eds.), *High-impact practices in online education*, (pp. 71–84). Sterling, VA: Stylus.

Ryan, M. (2012). Conceptualising and teaching discursive and performative reflection in higher education. *Studies in Continuing Education, 34*(2), 207–223.

Ryan, R. M, & Deci, E. L. (2000). *Self-determination theory and the facilitation of intrinsic motivation, social development, and well-being.* Available from https://selfdeterminationtheory.org/SDT/documents/2000_RyanDeci_SDT.pdf

Schroeder, C. (2011). *Coming in from the margins: Faculty development's emerging organizational development role in institutional change.* Sterling, VA: Stylus.

Spreitzer, G., Sutcliffe, K., Dutton, J., Sonenshein, S., & Grant, A. (2005). A socially embedded model of thriving at work. *Organization Science, 16*(5), 537–549.

Stahl, G., Koschmann, T., & Suthers, D. (2014). Computer-supported collaborative learning. In Sawyer, K. (Ed.), *The Cambridge handbook of the learning sciences* (pp. 461–478). New York, NY: Cambridge University Press.

University of North Carolina at Chapel Hill. (2010). *Online learning readiness questionnaire*. Available from https://www.unc.edu/tlim/ser/

UN News Centre. (2013). *Deputy UN chief calls for urgent action to tackle global sanitation crisis*. Available from http://www.un.org/apps/news/story.asp?NewsID=44452&Cr=sanitation&Cr1=#.WRxzX4jyuUn

U.S. Department of Education. (2010). *Evaluation of evidence-based practices in online learning: A meta-analysis and review of online learning studies*. Available from https://www2.ed.gov/rschstat/eval/tech/evidence-based-practices/finalreport.pdf

U.S. Department of Education. (2012). *Saint Mary-of-the-Woods College's administration of the Title IV programs: Final audit report*. Available from https://www2.ed.gov/about/offices/list/oig/auditreports/fy2012/a05k0012.pdf

U.S. News and World Report. (2018). *Methodology: Best online bachelor's programs rankings*. Available from https://www.usnews.com/education/online-education/articles/bachelors-methodology

ABOUT THE AUTHOR

Shannon Riggs has worked in higher education since 2001 and currently serves as executive director of course development and learning innovation for Oregon State University's Ecampus. Riggs is active nationally in the field of online education and is known for her commitment to quality and passion for supporting faculty.

Riggs regularly presents at conferences and has written for publication about online course development, faculty development, leadership, and innovation. She is currently serving a three-year elected position for the Quality Matters (QM) Instructional Design Association and a three-year elected position on the Western Interstate Commission for Higher Education Cooperative for Educational Technologies (WCET) Steering Committee.

INDEX

Online Learning books from Stylus Publishing

The Business of Innovating Online
Practical Tips and Advice from E-Learning Leaders
Edited by Kathryn E. Linder

Learning to Collaborate, Collaborating to Learn
Engaging Students in the Classroom and Online
Janet Salmons

Advancing Online Teaching
Creating Equity-Based Digital Learning Environments
Kevin Kelly and Todd D. Zakrajsek

High-Impact Practices in Online Education
Research and Best Practices
Edited by Kathryn E. Linder and
Chrysanthemum Mattison Hayes

Online Learning books from Stylus Publishing

Social Presence in Online Learning
Multiple Perspectives on Practice and Research
Edited by Aimee L. Whiteside, Amy Garrett Dikkers, and Karen Swan

How to Design and Teach a Hybrid Course
Achieving Student-Centered Learning through Blended Classroom, Online and Experiential Activities
Jay Caulfield

Discussion-Based Online Teaching To Enhance Student Learning
Theory Practice and Assessment
Tisha Bender

eService-Learning
Creating Experiential Learning and Civic Engagement Through Online and Hybrid Courses
Edited by Jean R. Strait and Katherine Nordyke

Teaching and Learning books from Stylus Publishing

Creating Wicked Students
Designing Courses for a Complex World
Paul Hanstedt

Dynamic Lecturing
Research-Based Strategies to Enhance Lecture Effectiveness
Christine Harrington and Todd Zakrajsek
Foreword by José Antonio Bowen

Creating Engaging Discussions
Strategies for "Avoiding Crickets" in Any Size Classroom and Online
Jennifer H. Herman and Linda B. Nilson
Foreword by Stephen D. Brookfield

Hitting Pause
65 Lecture Breaks to Refresh and Reinforce Learning
Gail Taylor Rice
Foreword by Kevin Barry

Teaching and Learning books from Stylus Publishing

Connected Teaching
Relationships, Power, and Mattering in Higher Education
Harriet L. Schwartz
Foreword by Laurent A. Daloz

POGIL
An Introduction to Process Oriented Guided Inquiry Learning for Those Who Wish to Empower Learners
Edited by Shawn R. Simonson

Teaching as the Art of Staging
A Scenario-Based College Pedagogy in Action
Anthony Weston
Foreword by Peter Felten

Project-Based Learning in the First Year
Beyond All Expectations
Edited by Kristin K. Wobbe and Elisabeth A. Stoddard
Foreword by Randall Bass

Jump-Start Your Online Classroom

Mastering Five Challenges in Five Days

David S. Stein and Constance E. Wanstreet

Jump-Start Your Online Classroom prepares a first-time online instructor to successfully manage the first few weeks of a course, including activities to help instructors plan, manage, and facilitate online instruction, and provides resources helpful during the beginning weeks of class. Each chapter is developed around the immediate challenges instructors face when teaching online. The authors address everyday problems and suggest solutions informed by their extensive research and experience.

The book is based on the authors' design and facilitation model, which identifies five elements comprising an online learning environment: digital tools, participants, social practices, learning community, and outcomes. The book shows how each aspect influences instructional practices and interacts to create an environment for a meaningful online educational experience.

22883 Quicksilver Drive
Sterling, VA 20166-2019

Subscribe to our e-mail alerts: www.Styluspub.com

The Blended Course Design Workbook

A Practical Guide

Kathryn E. Linder

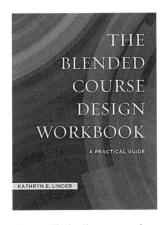

"Katie Linder has written a practical, smart, and even compassionate book on blended course design. Drawing on both research and experience, she walks readers through the process of creating blended courses that will challenge and engage students, providing plenty of examples and tips along the way. This is the essential guide we need to ensure our students will be successful in blended courses." —**Peter Felten**, *Assistant Provost for Teaching & Learning, Elon University*

The Blended Course Design Workbook meets the need for a user-friendly resource that provides faculty members and administrators with instructions, activities, tools, templates, and deadlines to guide them through the process of revising their traditional face-to-face course into a blended format. It includes detailed instructions for each stage of course design alongside specific activities that the reader can complete. The book is unique because it facilitates a step-by-step process for blended course design with specific templates and tools that can be used across disciplines.

(Continues on preceding page)

Also available from Stylus

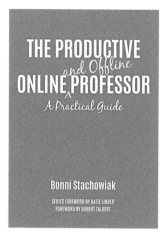

The Productive Online and Offline Professor

Bonni Stachowiak

Series Foreword by Kathryn E. Linder

Foreword by Robert Talbert

The author assists those who teach online and blended courses with managing their personal productivity, offering guidance and suggesting software tools for streamlining communication and productivity to enable faculty to better balance their lives while giving rich feedback to students.

This is a practical guide for how to provide high-quality online classes to today's diverse students. It is intended to be a professional resource for fulfilling our roles with excellence and joy, while managing other priorities in our personal and professional lives.

(Continues on preceding page)